Champneys COOKBOOK

Champneys COOKBOOK

ADAM PALMER

WITH PHOTOGRAPHS BY MARTIN BRIGDALE

BOXTREE

Acknowledgements

Thanks are due to Paula Gilbert, the Champneys dietician since 1988.
Paula has coordinated the analysis of the recipes in this book and works
closely with Adam and his team to advise on new dietary ideas and discuss
menus.

Thanks also to Tanya and Allan Wheway, Joint Managing Directors, and
to Gillie Turner, Deputy General Manager; Helena Champion, Consultant
Nutritionist; Christopher McLean, Sous Chef; Ian Bamford, Chef
Tournant; Jeremy Ginn, Chef de Partie; Edward Turner, Chef de Partie,
and Martin Turner, for their invaluable help in producing this book.

First published in 1993
by Boxtree Limited
Broadwall House
21 Broadwall
London SE1 9PL
United Kingdom

1 3 5 7 9 10 8 6 4 2

Text © Champneys 1993

Photographs © Martin Brigdale 1993

Styling by Cherry Ramseyer
with special thanks to Villeroy & Boch Tableware Ltd
and other manufacturers for providing tableware

Designed by David Rowley Design

Edited by Anness Publishing

Colour reproduction in Hong Kong by Fotographics

Typeset by SX Composing Ltd, Rayleigh, Essex

Printed and bound in Great Britain by Butler & Tanner, Frome

A CIP catalogue record for this book is available from the British Library.

ISBN 1-85283-407-2

Contents

Introduction 6

Cold Starters 14

Hot Starters 30

Fish & Seafood 50

Meat, Poultry & Game 66

Vegetable Dishes 90

Desserts 110

Basics 136

Menu Ideas 146

Glossary 152

Index 156

The Champneys Approach – a wholesome balance

WHEN Champneys started in 1925, the notion of promoting health was considered an oddity. Today, health is a word on everyone's lips, in every magazine, even on restaurant menus and the packages of many of the foods we buy. It has become an industry. Although this rise marks a vast improvement in people's eating habits, there are two risks: that we become blasé through overexposure and – an even greater danger – that we are swamped by an excess of conflicting advice.

Through all the fads and fashions, Champneys has consistently maintained and developed its straightforward approach to positive health through balanced eating. It has avoided extremes and concentrated on the gentler philosophy of moderation, common sense and enjoyment of food that anyone who has stayed at Champneys will have experienced firsthand in our restaurant.

Many people tend to think of healthy eating as a minefield of dos and don'ts, but food should be seen as something to be enjoyed as well as being good for you. Weight, shape and good health depend on what people eat and how much exercise they take. Using this book can help you to get the balance right. All the recipes have been specially created by our chef, Adam Palmer, and written in easy-to-follow stages. They cater for every occasion. Some can be made in a few minutes, while some are more complex and sophisticated dishes. There are many exciting new recipes to encourage a varied diet and also traditional favourites made with all the flavour, but using less fat and sugar.

Most of the recipes are designed to give four servings, but many can be adapted for smaller or larger quantities by decreasing or increasing all the ingredients accordingly. Calories per serving and basic nutritional information are given for each recipe, enabling you to plan a well-balanced diet. If you are on a weight-loss diet, we suggest you simply serve yourself smaller portions. Although many of the dishes are low in calories, there are also plenty for those who are not planning to lose weight. What the recipes have in common is that they are for people who want to be healthy, but who still want to enjoy their food. There is no secret to healthy eating, just the sensible application of some simple guidelines. Adopt them and you will soon start to feel better and lead a healthier, fuller life.

Ingredients

Fresh ingredients are always better than their frozen, tinned or otherwise processed counterparts. Of course, fresh foods are usually more expensive and often more trouble to prepare, but they are worth it. At Champneys, we believe the fresher the better, and many of the vegetables served in the restaurant are grown in our own kitchen garden. If you have a garden, the time and space, you may like to try growing some of your own vegetables too – it's an interesting and rewarding activity, as well as being good for you! At Champneys we use only fresh produce, but if a fresh ingredient eludes you,

Champneys health resort, set among beautiful grounds, is renowned for its elegance and style.

remember that frozen food often maintains more of its essential nutrients than other forms of processed food.

Eating a variety of foodstuffs is also important. This not only ensures a balanced intake of all the necessary nutrients, but also makes mealtimes so much more interesting. Some weight-loss diets in particular lack the variety to keep their adherents healthy and so should be avoided. If you eat properly you should not need vitamin supplements, especially if you make a point of not peeling vegetables and fruit unless it is necessary (many nutrients are in the skin or immediately beneath it). However, if you often eat vegetables that are cooked for a long time before you eat them and therefore subject to high vitamin loss, or if you smoke or drink regularly, are in ill health or pregnant, you may require a general multivitamin.

Quantities

The single biggest eating problem that we encounter at Champneys, and one that is so often ignored or overlooked, is that many of us simply eat too much. When shopping and preparing foods, gauge quantities carefully. Make serving the right quantity a part of presentation: a well-arranged plate is so much more attractive than one piled high. No meal should leave you feeling bloated: small, regular meals are better for you than large, occasional ones as they will keep your metabolic rate raised. Eat slowly. If you know you are going to eat a large meal – in a restaurant, or away from home where you are not in control of portions – try to compensate by cutting down the day before, which is much better than cutting down the day after, although this may not always be practicable.

High Fibre

Dietary fibre is essential in maintaining a healthy metabolism. It helps avoid constipation and other related Western diseases, such as haemorrhoids, varicose veins, diverticulitis and appendicitis. As well as being good for our digestive systems, fibre may also lower the amount of cholesterol in the blood. In addition, it helps us eat less calorie- or fat-rich food because its bulk fills us up. Choose wholewheat bread, flour and pasta and brown rice rather than their white counterparts. Pulses also offer high fibre and should appear regularly in your meals: lentils, split peas, kidney beans and so on. You may feel a little bloated if you eat more of these foods, but your digestion will soon adapt to the higher fibre intake. Ensure you soak and cook pulses properly, especially kidney beans, to prevent this occurring.

High Activity

Eating good, balanced meals every day is a vital step towards optimum health; regular exercise is another. However, when adding adequate exercise to your busy schedule, remember that an increase in physical activity means that you may need to increase your calorie intake to meet your additional energy expenditure. The best way to do this is to increase starch-based foods, such as bread, potatoes, pasta and rice. Do not eat a full meal immediately before or after exercising. Instead, choose a high-fibre, high-starch snack such as a banana, a slice of malt loaf, or wholewheat toast with sugar-free jam and no butter or margarine. (The fibre content controls the release of energy.) A little liquid before and after exercising is recommended. Select from tea, especially herb or fruit tea, decaffeinated coffee, skimmed milk drinks, diluted fruit juice or non-carbonated mineral water. Best of all is cool water. Remember that most people don't drink enough; aim for at least eight glasses of liquid per day.

Low Fat

Traditionally, diets have been measured by the number of calories consumed. Increasingly, however, the significance of calories is being replaced by that of fat. Too much fat – and most of us consume far too much – means an excess of calories as well as an increased risk of high blood cholesterol, high blood pressure and heart disease. Using the recipes in this book regularly should help you reduce your fat consumption, but in addition be aware of the fat content of all foods and control your fat intake carefully. Mono- and unsaturated oils are by far the best, e.g. olive, sesame and walnut. Olive-oil based margarines are actually better than poly- or saturated fat spreads and butter, and skimmed milk and low-fat cheeses are preferable to full-fat dairy products. As you will discover in this book, a wise option for making sauces is the use of low-fat yoghurt or *fromage frais* in place of the traditional cream and butter. Another good way to reduce your fat intake is to trim the skin and fat from poultry and red meat, or better still choose lower-fat options to red meat: venison and game, for example, or even the non-meat alternatives such as pulses. Remember that offal is inclined to be high in cholesterol and may have to be avoided by those suffering from high blood cholesterol. If you like gravy with your meat, add a few ice cubes before you finish cooking it. These attract the fat and can be immediately removed. When you put jam on bread or scrambled eggs on toast, the moistness of the topping means that you don't need the addition of a layer of butter or margarine. Finally, not all fats are bad for you! The oils in some fish, such as tuna, salmon and trout, have been proved to have beneficial qualities, and are believed to provide protection from coronary heart disease, as well as being a valuable source of calcium.

Low Salt

Most of us consume excessive amounts of salt in our food – this is especially true if you eat a lot of processed foods – and our palates have grown accustomed to high salt levels. Preparing our own fresh food has the additional value of allowing us to choose how much salt we add during cooking. Adding salt at the table is often no more than a habit we should curb. Too much salt is inclined to influence water retention and can be a cause of hypertension (high blood pressure).

Low Sugar

Refined sugar contains little more than calories. Honey is a more acceptable sweetener as it not only contains some useful minerals, but also fewer calories than sugar. Similarly, dried, fresh or frozen fruits make nutritious alternative sweeteners. Remember that processed drinks as well as food often contain high levels of sugar (as well as other unhealthy additives). Artificial sweeteners such as aspartame have negligible calories and are not dangerous to health in small amounts. If used in cooking, to sweeten stewed fruit, the flavour is better if added at the end.

Low Alcohol

For most of us small amounts of alcohol are a perfectly acceptable part of a healthy diet. Apart from being very enjoyable, a *little* wine can actually contribute to health by improving your circulation. However, remember that alcohol is high in calories, and that it should be treated with extreme caution if you are trying to lose weight. Although low-alcohol or alcohol-free wine is increasingly popular, it is not necessarily any lower in calories than its alcoholic equivalent. A better way of reducing both alcoholic and calorific intake is to make sure your wine glass contains a high proportion of mineral water. Don't shy away from cooking with wine: it can improve the flavour of a dish and heating to boiling point causes the alcohol and some calories to evaporate, leaving just the taste.

Appearances are important!

How food is presented is vital to its success. If a dish looks appetizing, it is far more likely to taste good! The photographs in this book will give you ideas on how to present the dishes, but do use your imagination and experiment. Bear in mind all the elements that influence the appearance of your dish: the colour, texture and shape (if any) of the food itself; the table setting, décor and flowers; the occasion; the available garnishes, and even the plate on which the dish will be served. When using flowers for garnishing, first establish that they are not poisonous and that they have not been sprayed with anything toxic. Roses, violets, nasturtiums, marigolds and borage are all fine, as long as they are washed carefully.

Special Diets

If you are taking medication or have any health concerns it is wise to consult your doctor before embarking on a diet.

Anaemia Sufferers

It is important to take a source of vitamin C with all meals to aid iron absorption. This could take the form of a glass of tomato juice, some fresh orange juice, a couple of kiwi fruits or even new potatoes cooked in their skins.

Arthritis Sufferers

To help relieve the pain associated with arthritis, it is advisable to avoid citrus fruits, red meat and raw tomatoes.

Gluten-free diets

Coeliac disease or grain allergy force some people to adopt a diet that is free of gluten, a constituent of wheat, rye, barley and oats. Wheat allergy can cause such symptoms as abdominal bloating, discomfort and weight gain. Avoiding wheat is actually quite difficult, as flour is used in a high proportion of dishes and processed foods, for example as a thickener – it can even be found in baked beans! When cooking gluten-free, remember that you should use cornflour or cornstarch, or arrowroot rather than conventional thickening agents.

As Master of Cuisine at Champneys, Adam Palmer creates a truly innovative range of delicious, exotic yet healthy dishes.

Vegetarian Diets

There has been a well-publicized move towards vegetarianism over recent years and health has been one of the main motives. From the vegan, who eats no meat, fish or dairy products, to the 'occasional' meat eater, there are many shades of vegetarianism. As a reaction against the standard Western diet many people are now lowering their meat consumption, which is definitely a move in the right direction. Animal products generally contain high proportions of saturated fats as well as protein, and we are inclined to consume too much of both of them. However, to say that vegetarianism is healthy is a dangerous generalization. It can be, so long as you ensure that your diet gives you the wide variety of nutrients that you need. Bear in mind that dairy products can contain even more saturated fat and protein than meat. If you do decide to go vegan, ensure that you eat enough protein; you need 2 sources of vegetable protein in each meal. A variety of vegetables, grains, fruit and nuts can give you all the necessary vitamins and minerals to keep you healthy, but may not give you adequate calcium, iron or vitamins D and B_{12}. Remember that lacto-vegetarian cooking is inclined to be high in calories, especially when ingredients like full-fat cheese and nuts are used in large quantities.

Most of us obtain our calcium from dairy products, but the alternative sources, although not as rich, are nuts, pulses, green leafy vegetables, figs and hard water. Vegans are recommended to drink vegetable milk fortified with calcium. Iron is abundantly present in meat and offal, but alternatives include green leafy vegetables, pulses, seeds, eggs and dried apricots. Vitamin C aids the absorption of iron, as described in the section for anaemics above. Vitamin D is obtained from sunlight, so in winter or during a typical British summer this may need to be supplemented with foods rich in the vitamin. Most of us can obtain it from oily fish, eggs and yoghurt, but vegans may have to rely on fortified foods, such as some margarines and breakfast cereals. Vitamin B_{12} is present in eggs and dairy products, so vegans should take care to have this in the form of yeast extracts, soya milk or some breakfast cereals fortified with B_{12}.

Weight-loss Diets

If your diet is for the purpose of losing weight, it is important to decide at the start how much you plan to lose over a particular period of time and to make these aims realistic. Rather than rely on charts that show what your weight should be in proportion to your height, it is sometimes better to aim for a weight suitable for your age, based on your starting weight at 18 years old if you felt happy with this weight. To lose 450 g/1 lb you will need to reduce your calorific intake by 3500 per week. A good guideline is to aim to lose 1-1.15 kg/2-2½ lb a week, which means that if your normal daily intake is 2000 calories, you will need to reduce this to 1000. It is important to remember that the more slowly you lose weight, the more likely you are to maintain the loss. Once you have reached your target weight, a good way to prevent the weight from coming back on is to maintain your special diet effectively from Monday to Thursday or Friday and then eat normally over the weekend.

Men are inclined to lose weight at a steadier and faster rate than women, due to their lower percentage of body fat and the lack of hormonal influences. Women, after losing weight steadily, will often reach a 'plateau' for 3 or 4 days when their weight remains the same. Although this is dispiriting for even the most determined dieter, it is often only a temporary halt, simply due to fluid fluctuations. Do not give up – the weight should then start to fall again.

Many of the recipes in this book can be incorporated in a weight-loss diet and the calorific value of each dish is indicated. We base our recipes on a daily energy intake of 1000 calories for women and 1200 for men. It is important to establish good eating habits at the start of your diet and to maintain them even after you have completed it and reached your target weight.

You will lose weight more easily if you cut out alcohol altogether during your diet, but many people find this difficult to do. Cut down by drinking single measures rather than doubles, or by alternating between alcohol and a low-calorie non-alcoholic alternative, and reserve at least 2 alcohol-free days a week.

A simple way to help you lose weight, as well as helping to keep you healthy, is to make sure that you drink plenty of water. Between 1-1.5 litres/1¾-2½ pints – 3¾-6½ cups is the recommended daily intake and many people fail to drink this quantity. Water taken with meals not only aids digestion but also has the effect of filling you up and limiting your appetite. Clear soup acts in much the same way, but avoid the accompanying bread roll. Also, remember to take time to enjoy your food – by eating slowly you will often satisfy your hunger before you have finished everything on your plate.

Avoiding the baddies

Many people suffer cravings for foods that are bad for them. This often occurs mid-afternoon, when a drop in blood sugar level has people reaching for fattening foods. Chocolate is among the most common of these. The craving may not only be for the obvious sugar content of the chocolate, but also for the stimulant caffeine. Caffeine contains a chemical called theobromine which gives chocoholics the buzz they seek. Giving up chocolate can be difficult and the healthy alternative of fresh fruit is rarely an acceptable substitute for serious addicts, so some self-discipline is required. Bananas may be a good 'non-fattening' alternative and each one will keep blood sugar levels up for approximately 4 hours while being only 15 calories more than an apple.

The Champneys Way
Sensible eating as part of a healthy lifestyle

In 1925, Stanley Lief, a Russian Jew who had trained in naturopathy in the United States, bought the estate of Champneys and turned it into England's first health resort. Lief had had remarkable success, treating patients suffering from ailments that traditional medicine had failed to cure. Champneys was soon discovered by British society and Lief was lionized as the new leader of alternative medicine in this country.

The secret of Lief's success may have been simpler than anyone suspected at the time. In the 1920s the rich and leisured classes who came to Champneys knew nothing of healthy eating. They consumed too much of everything, especially sugars and fats, resulting in a whole range of diseases, from depression and nervous ailments to skin diseases, asthma, colitis, peptic ulcers and coronary heart disease, and there were few of the drugs that are available today to treat these conditions. A key element of the naturopathic philosophy is fasting and today it is thought that many of Stanley Lief's 'miracle cures' of the 1920s and 1930s may have been attributable to an improvement in health brought about by simply denying patients their customary excesses.

Together with sensible eating, the Champneys way advises an overall healthy lifestyle, including having proper exercise, learning and using strategies to cope with stress and developing a positive approach to life. As well as being a wonderful experience, staying at Champneys is not an isolated holiday away from bad habits, but the start of a new, improved lifestyle for all our guests.

The first Champneys cookbook was published in 1987 in response to many requests for recipes from guests who wanted to cook dishes served in our restaurant in their own homes. Its success and enquiries about new recipes have inspired this new issue. The Champneys team, and especially chef Adam Palmer, wish you happy cooking, *bon appétit* and the very best of health.

Cold starters

provide a wide range of light and healthy dishes from simple salads of Asparagus and Potato Mayonnaise to the exotic flavours of Salmon and Leek Mousse with Salmon Roe Sauce, and Chicken, Venison and Wild Mushroom Terrine. Choose colours, textures and garnishes appropriate to the meal.

Lobster and Red Pepper Mousse

4 red peppers
2 dsp olive oil
2 shallots, chopped
2 medium tomatoes, roughly
   chopped
2 tsp raspberry vinegar
6 sheets gelatine
550 g/1¼ lb whole cooked lobster
400 ml/14 fl oz/¾ cup natural, low-
   fat *fromage frais*

Vinaigrette
2 very ripe tomatoes
2 dsp white wine vinegar
75 ml/3 fl oz/⅓ cup olive oil
sea salt and freshly milled black
   pepper

Garnish
4 sprigs chervil (optional)

Serves 4

Chop 3 of the red peppers into rough dice. Heat a dessertspoon of the olive oil in a small frying pan (skillet) and sweat the peppers and shallots until the shallots are translucent. Add the roughly chopped tomatoes and the raspberry vinegar and reduce by half over a high heat. Remove from the heat.

Meanwhile, cover the sheet gelatine with cold water and leave to soften for approximately 5 minutes. Remove from the water with your hand and squeeze out any excess liquid, then place the gelatine in a small heatproof bowl over a pan of barely simmering water. Leave until the gelatine has melted and turned transparent.

Thoroughly stir the gelatine into the contents of the pan, then transfer the mixture to a food processor or blender and blend thoroughly. Press through a fine sieve into a clean bowl and leave to cool.

Remove the tail flesh and claw flesh from the lobster. Cut the tail meat into thin collops and reserve for garnishing. Chop up the claw meat and add the red pepper purée, then fold in the *fromage frais* and lightly season. Spoon the mixture into 4 ramekins and leave in the refrigerator for at least 2 hours to set.

To make the vinaigrette, put the tomatoes and the vinegar in a food processor or blender, lightly season and blend until smooth. Add the olive oil, pass through a fine sieve and check the seasoning. Correct the consistency with a little water if the dressing is too thick.

Peel the remaining pepper and cut into fine dice; reserve for garnishing..

To serve, place a quarter of the lobster collops in the centre of each plate to form a bed. Briefly plunge each ramekin up to the rim in hot water, invert and place a mousse on top of the collops. Spoon round diced peppers and tomato vinaigrette and top with a sprig of chervil, if liked.

Fat: high Kcals: 405 Cholesterol: medium Fibre: medium

Clockwise, from top: *Asparagus and Potato Mayonnaise, Crab, Beetroot and Apple Salad, and Lobster and Red Pepper Mousse*

Crab, Beetroot and Apple Salad

½ cooked beetroot (beet)

1 tbsp clear honey

3 tbsp cider vinegar

1 green apple

1 red apple

1 bunch chives, half finely chopped,
     half cut into batons

1 tbsp extra virgin olive oil

juice of 1 lime

225 g/8 oz white crab meat

3 tbsp natural, low-fat *fromage frais*

sea salt and freshly milled black
     pepper

Garnish

4 sprigs chervil

Serves 4

Square off the beetroot and cut into neat batons, reserving the trimmings. Purée the trimmings with the honey and cider vinegar in a food processor or blender and squeeze through a fine sieve. Reserve the juice for a dressing.

Chop the apples into small dice, leaving on the peel. Mix the puréed beetroot with half the chopped chives and half the apple then stir in a tablespoon of olive oil, the lime juice and the crab meat.

To serve, push a quarter of the crab meat mixture into a 6 cm/2½ in circular pastry cutter, pressing down firmly, and place in the centre of the plate. Carefully remove the cutter and repeat for each serving. Season the *fromage frais* and spread on top of each crab circle. Arrange beetroot batons around the crab, crisscross with chive batons, garnish with chervil. Whisk the remaining olive oil with the beetroot juice and pour over the crab.

Fat: medium Kcals: 165 Cholesterol: medium Fibre: low

Asparagus and Potato Mayonnaise

350 g/12 oz potatoes, roughly
     chopped

½ tsp truffle oil

3 fresh basil leaves

juice of 1 lemon

4 tbsp extra virgin olive oil

28 asparagus spears

2 truffles, sliced

sea salt and freshly milled white
     pepper

Serves 4

Boil the potatoes in a little salted water until soft. Drain, then place in a food processor or liquidizer with the truffle oil, basil and lemon juice and process until smooth. Slowly add the olive oil, drop by drop, with the machine turned on. Adjust the seasoning with salt and white pepper to taste. Place the mayonnaise in the refrigerator to cool.

Cut away the woody ends from the asparagus spears and trim to the same length; the stalks of older, fatter asparagus will need to be thinly peeled. Tie into 4 bundles of 7 and blanch in boiling water for 3 minutes. Refresh under cold running water, then drain. Leave to cool.

To serve, place a bundle of asparagus in the centre of each plate and discard the strings. Spoon over a little mayonnaise and top with a few slices of truffle.

Fat: high Kcals: 235 Cholesterol: low Fibre: medium

Chicken Leek Mousse with Beetroot Salad

10 baby leeks, blanched and cut
    into strips
2 × 170g/6 oz breasts of corn-fed
    chicken, skinned, boned and
    trimmed
575 ml/20 fl oz/2½ cups chicken
    stock (see page 138)
3 sheets gelatine
2 tbsp natural, low-fat *fromage frais*
1 small beetroot (beet), cooked and
    cut into 2.5 cm/1 in batons,
    reserving trimmings
2 tbsp cider vinegar
1 tbsp extra virgin olive oil
1 bunch chives, cut into 2.5 cm/1 in
    batons
sea salt and chilli pepper

Serves 4

Line 4 ramekins with strips of leek. Poach the chicken breasts in the stock in a covered pan for 10 minutes.

Meanwhile, cover the sheet gelatine with cold water and leave to soften for approximately 5 minutes. Remove from the water with your hand and squeeze out any excess liquid, then place the gelatine in a small heatproof bowl. Put the bowl into a pan of barely simmering water and leave until the gelatine has melted and turned transparent.

Transfer the cooked chicken breasts to a food processor or blender, add the *fromage frais*, seasonings and the gelatine and process until smooth. Press through a fine sieve and spoon the mousse into the ramekins. Leave in the refrigerator for 1 hour.

To make the dressing, liquidize the beetroot trimmings with the cider vinegar and the olive oil in a liquidizer or food processor.

To serve, plunge the base of each ramekin up to the rim into hot water for 30 seconds and then turn out into the centre of each plate, arrange the beetroot (beet) batons and chives around, and spoon over the dressing.

Fat: medium Kcals: 134 Cholesterol: low Fibre: low

Sardine and Red Onion Terrine

900 g/2 lb fresh sardines, filleted
    and washed
2 tbsp wholemeal flour
2 large red onions, sliced
3 tbsp extra virgin olive oil
4 tbsp red wine vinegar

Sauce
1 tbsp capers
1 tbsp pickled gherkin slices
1 tbsp black olives, pitted
sea salt and freshly milled black
    pepper

Serves 14

Lightly flour the sardine fillets and season with salt and pepper.

Sauté the sliced onion in a pan with 1 tablespoon of the olive oil over a low heat for 5 minutes until golden brown. Deglaze with 1 tablespoon of the vinegar. Remove the onion mixture from the pan and set aside. In the same pan, heat 2 tablespoons of the olive oil until smoking, then quickly fry the floured fillets until golden brown.

Line a 1.1 litre/2 pint/5 cup terrine with cling film or plastic wrap and place a layer of fillets on the base, followed by a layer of onions. Continue the layers until the terrine is full. Pour over the remaining vinegar, wrap cling film or plastic wrap over the top and press with a heavy weight or dish filled with cold water for at least 3 hours in the refrigerator.

Liquidize the capers, gherkin slices and olives in a liquidizer or food processor together with the remaining olive oil. Invert the terrine onto a dish or board, remove the plastic and cut into 2 cm/¾ in slices. Serve with the sauce.

Fat: medium Kcals: 135 Cholesterol: medium Fibre: low

Mackerel, Rhubarb and Mange-Tout Terrine

4 new potatoes

2 pinches saffron powder

wholemeal flour, for coating

16 × 85 g/3 oz fillets of mackerel

1 tbsp extra virgin olive oil

10 sticks rhubarb

170 g/6 oz/1 cup mange-tout (sugar
    snap peas), blanched

juice of 1 lemon

3 tbsp red wine vinegar

150 ml/¼ pt/⅔ cup white wine

1 tbsp clear honey

4 chives, chopped

sea salt and freshly milled black
    pepper

Serves 14

Preheat the oven to 150°C/300°F/gas 2. Line a 1.1 litre/2 pint/5 cup terrine with greaseproof (wax) paper. Leave the skins on the potatoes and cut into thin slices. Cook in lightly salted water with a pinch of saffron powder. Drain and leave to cool.

Season the flour, and use to coat the mackerel fillets. Heat the olive oil in a pan then fry the fillets for about 3 minutes until nearly cooked, turning once halfway through.

Cut 8 sticks of rhubarb to fit the length of the terrine and place in a roasting tray. Bake in the oven for 5 minutes until slightly softened.

Blanch the mange-tout (sugar snap peas) in lightly salted water for 1 minute, then drain and refresh under cold running water.

Layer the terrine with the mackerel fillets, baked rhubarb, mange-tout (sugar snap peas) and the slices of potato, alternating the vegetables between the layers of fish. When the terrine is full pour a little lemon juice on top and place the terrine upside on a clean tray to catch the juices. Refrigerate with a heavy weight or dish filled with cold water on top for 3–4 hours.

Cut the remaining sticks of rhubarb into 6 cm/2½ in batons and poach in the vinegar until soft. Drain and allow to cool.

When the terrine is ready, pour any juices that have run off into a pan, add the white wine, honey and a pinch of saffron powder and reduce over a high heat by half. Allow to cool.

To serve, place the terrine upside down on a serving plate and gently remove the mould, carefully peeling away the greaseproof (wax) paper. Surround with the chives and the rhubarb batons.

Fat: high Kcals: 396 Cholesterol: high Fibre: low

Wild Mushroom and Chicken Terrine

200 g/7 oz breast meat of corn-fed
    chicken, skinned, boned and
    trimmed

1 tsp extra virgin olive oil

1 onion, finely chopped

1 clove garlic, finely diced (minced)

50 g/2 oz oyster mushrooms, finely
    diced (minced)

100 ml/4 fl oz/½ cup white wine

1 tbsp powdered gelatine

1 sprig tarragon, roughly chopped

Chop the chicken breasts into 2.5 cm/1 in cubes. Heat the olive oil in a pan until smoking, then add the chicken, chopped onion, garlic and the oyster mushrooms. Cook for 5 minutes over a low heat until the onion is translucent.

Place the wine in a small heatproof bowl, sprinkle over the gelatine and leave it to go spongy. Place the bowl in a pan of barely simmering water and leave until the gelatine has melted and turned transparent. Stir into the pan containing the diced chicken breasts and add the tarragon. Increase the heat and reduce the liquid by two-thirds, then blend the contents of the pan in a food processor or blender together with the *fromage frais* until smooth. Spoon into a 575 ml/1 pint/2½ cup terrine mould and place in the refrigerator to set for 1 hour.

Mackerel, Rhubarb and Mange-Tout Terrine

1 tbsp natural, low-fat *fromage frais*
poppy seeds
sea salt and freshly milled black
　pepper

Garnish
lettuce leaves, roughly torn

Serves 10

To turn out the mould, plunge the terrine up to its rim in hot water for 30 seconds. Place a plate upside down on the mould, then turn both over and give a couple of sharp shakes. Carefully roll the terrine in the poppy seeds, then cut into 1 cm/½ in slices. Serve the sliced terrine on a serving platter garnished with torn lettuce leaves.

Fat: low Kcals: 29 Cholesterol: low Fibre: low

Melon Lime Soup

juice of 3 limes
1 tsp arrowroot
2 egg whites
2 overripe Ogen or Galia melons

Serves 4

Mix the arrowroot to a paste with a little water and stir into the lime juice. Place in a stainless steel saucepan and bring to the boil, stirring continuously. Remove from the heat.

In a clean, dry bowl, whisk the egg whites until stiff and gently fold into the thickened lime juice using a large metal spoon. Place in the freezer for 3 hours.

Halve the melons and discard the seeds. Scoop out the flesh into a food processor or blender and purée. Chill in the refrigerator for 30 minutes. Serve in chilled soup bowls with a scoop of frozen lime.

Fat: low Kcals: 86 Cholesterol: low Fibre: low

Marinated Sea Bass with Pickled Vegetables

4 × 115 g/4 oz fillets of sea bass

Marinade
½ tsp fenugreek
2 star anise
1 tsp coriander seeds
½ tsp white peppercorns
juice of 2 limes
1 tsp cider vinegar
3 tbsp white wine
6 sprigs parsley
1 bay leaf
1 small red chilli
½ tsp mustard seeds
2 dsp extra virgin olive oil

Pickled vegetables
150 ml/5 fl oz/⅔ cup cider vinegar
3 tbsp clear honey
1 pinch saffron powder
8 baby courgettes (zucchini)
32 assorted baby root vegetables
8 baby green tomatoes
sea salt and freshly milled black
    pepper

Serves 4

Mix all the marinade ingredients together. Place the sea bass fillets in a shallow dish and spoon over the marinade and leave for 2 hours in the refrigerator.

Meanwhile, place the cider vinegar and honey in a pan, season, and bring to the boil. Add all the baby vegetables and the saffron, and boil for one minute. Leave the vegetables to stand in the liquid until cold.

Drain the sea bass from the marinade and place under a hot grill until just cooked, 4–5 minutes.

To serve, place a sea bass fillet in the centre of each plate and surround with a selection of baby vegetables. Spoon over some of the pickling liquid onto the vegetables and a trickle of olive oil.

Fat: low Kcals: 201 Cholesterol: medium Fibre: medium

Champneys Gazpacho

100 g/3½ oz/½ cup onions, roughly chopped
100 g/3½ oz/¾ cup cucumber, roughly chopped
100 g/3½ oz/¾ cup red and green peppers, roughly chopped
575 ml/1 pt/2½ cups tomato juice
75 ml/3 fl oz/⅓ cup fresh orange juice
1 dash lemon juice
55 g/2 oz/⅓ cup fresh breadcrumbs
1 dash red wine vinegar
1 clove garlic, finely diced (minced)
sea salt and freshly milled black pepper

Garnish
4 tbsp mixed peppers, finely diced (minced)

Serves 4

Put all the ingredients, except for the diced peppers for the garnish, in a food processor or liquidizer and process until well blended. Chill in the refrigerator and serve cold, garnished with the diced peppers.

Fat: low Kcals: 88 Cholesterol: low Fibre: low

Basmati Rice Timbale with Coriander, Truffle and Pineapple Dressing

2 dsp extra virgin olive oil

170 g/6 oz wild mushrooms

1 shallot, chopped

175 ml/6 fl oz/¾ cup unsweetened apple juice

55 g/2 oz/⅓ cup pineapple, finely diced (minced), reserving stalk

½ tsp truffle oil

1 stem ginger, finely chopped

1 clove garlic, finely diced (minced)

1 fresh green chilli

1 tbsp white wine vinegar

1 egg white

1 tsp fresh coriander, chopped

juice of 1 lime

200 g/7 oz/¾ cup cooked brown basmati rice

6 tbsp natural, low-fat *fromage frais*

10 chives, finely chopped

sea salt and fresh black pepper

Serves 4

Heat half the olive oil in a small frying pan (skillet) and sweat the wild mushrooms with the shallots until the shallots are translucent. Leave to cool.

To make the dressing, place the apple juice, remaining olive oil, pineapple and stalk, truffle oil, ginger, garlic, chilli and vinegar in a separate pan and reduce over a high heat by two-thirds. Leave to cool. Strain the liquid and set aside the diced (minced) pineapple.

Whisk the egg white until stiff, gently fold into the cooled dressing, then add the coriander and lime juice.

Mix the cooked rice with the diced pineapple and add 2 tablespoons of the *fromage frais*. Season to taste, then stir in half the mushroom and shallot mixture. Divide the mixture into 4, then press each portion into a 6 cm/2½ in circular pastry cutter, pushing down firmly. Remove the cutter to leave a rice timbale.

Stir the chopped chives into the remaining *fromage frais*, season to taste, then spread a little on top of each timbale, using a flat knife. Place a timbale in the centre of each plate and garnish with the pineapple dressing and serve.

Fat: medium Kcals: 157 Cholesterol: low Fibre: low

Above: *Smoked Haddock Tartare with Artichoke Terrine and Lemon Balm Dressing;* opposite, from back: *Basmati Rice Timbale with Coriander, Truffle and Pineapple Dressing, and Salmon and Leek Mousse with Salmon Roe Sauce*

Smoked Haddock Tartare with Artichoke Terrine and Lemon Balm Dressing

350 g/12 oz Jerusalem artichokes,
  thinly sliced
1 dash lemon juice
1 bunch flowering thyme

Haddock Tartare
170 g/6 oz natural smoked
  haddock, skinned and boned
4 garlic chives, chopped
2 shallots, chopped
juice of 1 lime
1 dsp raw cane sugar
4 tbsp natural, low-fat *fromage frais*
1 pinch sea salt

Spiced sultanas
85 g/3 oz/⅓ cup sultanas
1 pinch ground ginger
1 pinch ground cumin
1 pinch ground coriander
2 cloves
1 clove garlic
1 pinch cayenne pepper

Sauce
1 lemon
1 bunch lemon balm
6 tbsp extra virgin olive oil
1 tsp clear honey
1 pinch cayenne pepper
sea salt and freshly milled black
  pepper

Garnish
selection of salad leaves (e.g. lollo
  rosso, radicchio, endive, rocket)
1 tsp extra virgin olive oil
sea salt and freshly milled black
  pepper

Serves 4

Line a 2.5 cm × 5 cm/1 in × 2 in terrine with cling film or plastic wrap.

To make the spiced sultanas, put all the ingredients in a pan, just cover with water and bring to the boil. Cover and continue boiling until the sultanas are plump, about 20 minutes. Add more water if the sultanas start to dry out. When plump, drain and set aside.

In a pan, cover the sliced artichokes with water, the thyme and a dash of lemon juice, bring to the boil and simmer until soft, about 15 minutes.

Arrange thin layers of artichokes and sultanas in the terrine. Cover with greaseproof (wax) paper and press with a heavy weight or dish filled with cold water for 4 hours in the refrigerator.

Cut the smoked haddock into 2 mm/⅟₁₆ in dice and place in a shallow dish. Mix together the chopped chives and shallots and mix with the lime juice, sugar, yoghurt and sea salt. Spoon over the haddock and leave to marinate for 1 hour in the refrigerator. Turn the fish over after 30 minutes.

Invert the terrine onto a dish or serving board and roll it in the thyme flowers. Cut into thin slices.

Drain the marinated fish, divide into 4 portions and push into a 4 cm/1½ in circular pastry cutter to form a round cake. Remove the cutter and spread the top of the cake with the yoghurt marinade.

Wash the salad leaves and arrange them to one side of the fish cake. Season with a little olive oil, salt and pepper and add a slice of terrine to the plate.

To make the sauce, purée a whole lemon with the lemon balm leaves, olive oil, honey, salt and cayenne pepper in a liquidizer or food processor; pass through a fine sieve and pour around the terrine.

Fat: high Kcals: 414 Cholesterol: low Fibre: low

Chicken, Venison and Wild Mushroom Terrine

veal stock (see page 139), using
    1.75 l/3 pt water, 900 g/2 lb
    venison bones
6 medium-sized onions, finely
    chopped
1 medium-sized carrot, finely
    chopped
3 sticks celery, finely chopped
115 g /4 oz venison, minced
    (ground)
4 egg whites
50 ml/2 fl oz/¼ cup port
1½ heaped tsp powdered gelatine
3 × 170 g/6 oz breasts of corn-fed
    chicken, skinned, boned and
    trimmed
2 tbsp natural, low-fat *fromage frais*
2 tsp extra virgin olive oil
1 clove garlic, finely diced (minced)
225 g/8 oz mixed wild mushrooms,
    wiped
75 ml/3 fl oz/⅓ cup white wine
2 × 115 g/4 oz fillets of venison
1 cucumber, cut into batons,
    5 cm/2 in × 3 mm/⅛ in
sea salt, freshly milled white and
    black pepper

Garnish
1 bunch chervil

Serves 14

Reduce the veal stock over a high heat by two-thirds, then leave to cool. Mix 4 chopped onions, the carrot and celery with the minced (ground) venison. As soon as the stock has cooled, stir in 2 egg whites and add the minced (ground) venison mixture and the port. Bring the stock to the boil, then cover and simmer for 45 minutes over a very low heat.

About 10 minutes before the end of the cooking time, sprinkle the powdered gelatine over a small amount of cold water and leave to soften for approximately 5 minutes until it has swelled. Place the gelatine in a small heatproof bowl and put the bowl into a pan of barely simmering water; leave until the gelatine has melted and become transparent.

Strain the cooked stock through fine muslin, being careful not to cloud the stock. Season with salt and freshly milled white pepper, then stir in the gelatine and cool in a dampened shallow tray in the refrigerator. When the mixture has cooled, turn out onto a piece of dampened greaseproof (wax) paper and cut into 6 mm/¼ in dice using a sharp dampened knife, and return to the refrigerator.

Meanwhile, combine the chicken breasts, the remaining egg whites and the *fromage frais* in a food processor or blender and process until smooth. Season to taste.

Heat the oil in a frying pan (skillet) and sweat the remaining onion with the garlic and the wild mushrooms until the onions are translucent. Pour in the white wine. Allow to cool, then blend with the chicken mousse and press through a fine sieve. Keep cool.

Preheat the oven to 150°C/300°F/gas 2. Grease a 1.1 litre/2 pint/5 cup terrine with olive oil and line with greaseproof (wax) paper.

Seal the venison fillets in a very hot non-stick pan for 1 minute on each side. Spread a third of the chicken mousse in the base of the terrine, then lay one of the venison fillets on top. Add another layer of chicken mousse, followed by the remaining venison fillet. Cover with the last third of chicken mousse. Bake the terrine in a *bain marie* in the oven for 25 minutes. Remove and allow to cool.

Cut carefully around the edges of the terrine using a sharp knife and plunge the base in hot water up to its rim for 30 seconds. Turn out the terrine onto an inverted plate and cut into 1 cm/½ in slices. Arrange on individual plates with a little chopped veal aspic and cucumber batons and garnish with chervil leaves.

Fat: low Kcals: 126 Cholesterol: low Fibre: low

Swiss Chard, Beetroot, Avocado and Pecan Nut Salad

170 g/6 oz beetroot (beet)

8 leaves Swiss chard, finely
   shredded

30 g/1 oz/¼ cup pecan nuts

1 ripe avocado, peeled, stoned and
   sliced

Dressing

1 red pepper, deseeded and
   roughly chopped

2 tbsp walnut oil

1 tbsp white wine vinegar

Serves 4

To make the dressing, purée the pepper, walnut oil and white wine vinegar in a food processor or liquidizer and pass through a fine sieve.

Cook the beetroot (beet) until soft in a little water in a non-stick pan over a high heat, approximately 30 minutes. Refresh under cold running water, peel and cut into 6 mm/¼ in squares. Mix the shredded Swiss chard and the pecan nuts with the beetroot (beet) in a large salad bowl. Toss with a quarter of the dressing. Arrange the sliced avocado on top, pour over the remaining dressing and serve.

Fat: high Kcals: 206 Cholesterol: low Fibre: medium

Above: *Chicken, Venison and Wild Mushroom Terrine;* opposite: *Marinated Sea Bass with Pickled Vegetables*

Leek, Smoked Goat's Cheese and Sesame Seed Salad

2 leeks, sliced
55 g/2 oz/1 cup smoked goat's
    cheese, cut into ¼ in dice
110 g/4 oz new potatoes, cooked
    and sliced thinly
115 g/4 oz/1 cup cherry tomatoes
1 bunch dill

Dressing
55 g/2 oz bean curd
1 tsp whole grain mustard
1 tbsp toasted sesame oil
1 tsp tahini paste
1 tbsp white wine vinegar

Garnish
1 dsp toasted sesame seeds

Serves 4

To make the dressing, place the bean curd, mustard, sesame oil, tahini paste and white wine vinegar in a food processor or blender and blend until smooth. Press through a fine sieve. Place all the other ingredients, except the sesame seeds, into a large serving bowl. Mix in the dressing, garnish with the sesame seeds and serve.

Fat: medium Kcals: 119 Cholesterol: low Fibre: low

Salmon and Leek Mousse with Salmon Roe Sauce

2 tbsp white wine vinegar
3 × 85 g/3 oz fillets of fresh salmon
20 baby leeks, cut into 7.5 cm/3 in
    lengths
juice of ½ lemon
2 tbsp natural, low-fat *fromage frais*
1 dsp low-fat mayonnaise
1 pinch cayenne pepper
3 sheets gelatine
2 egg whites
15 g/½ oz/¼ cup salmon roe
sea salt

Serves 4

Bring a large pan of water to the boil, add the vinegar and poach the salmon for 4 minutes. Remove from the pan and leave to cool.

Blanch the leeks in lightly salted water, refresh under cold running water and drain. Line 4 ramekins with the leeks, alternating the strips.

Reserve a little lemon juice to mix with the salmon roe later and combine the rest with the salmon, *fromage frais*, a pinch each of salt and cayenne pepper and the mayonnaise in a food processor or blender.

Cover the gelatine with cold water and leave to soften, approximately 5 minutes. Remove from the water and squeeze out any excess liquid using your hand. Put the gelatine in a small heatproof bowl over a pan of barely simmering water and leave to melt.

Whisk the egg whites until stiff and fold into the salmon mousse together with the gelatine. Pour the mousse into the lined ramekins and place in the refrigerator for 30 minutes to set.

Mix half the roe with the reserved lemon juice and press firmly through a fine sieve into a clean bowl. Add the remaining roe and mix in. Plunge the base of each ramekin into hot water for 30 seconds and turn out onto serving plates. Pour sauce around each mousse.

Fat: high Kcals: 202 Cholesterol: medium Fibre: medium

Sweet Pepper, Chicken, Pineapple and Chilli Salad

2 × 140 g/5 oz breasts of corn-fed
    chicken, skinned, boned and
    trimmed
300 ml/10 fl oz/1¼ cups chicken
    stock (see page 138)
¼ pineapple, cut into 6 mm/¼ in
    dice
1 red pepper, deseeded and finely
    chopped
1 yellow pepper, deseeded and
    finely chopped
1 green pepper, deseeded and
    finely chopped
55 g/2 oz/⅓ cup bean sprouts
sea salt and freshly milled black
    pepper

Dressing
2 tbsp low-calorie mayonnaise
juice of 1 lemon
1 pinch ground cumin
1 pinch paprika
1 pinch ground turmeric
½ clove garlic, finely diced (minced)
½ bunch fresh coriander
1 red chilli pepper, deseeded and
    finely diced

Serves 4

Poach the chicken breasts in the chicken stock for 10 minutes, then remove and drain on kitchen paper.

Mix together the mayonnaise and lemon juice and add a pinch of cumin, paprika and turmeric and the garlic. Stir in half the chopped coriander and then the chilli pepper. Season to taste.

Cut the chicken into strips and in a large serving bowl mix with the pineapple, peppers and bean sprouts. Stir in the dressing and garnish with the remaining coriander.

Fat: medium Kcals: 169 Cholesterol: medium Fibre: low

Hot starters offer a wide range of healthy and delicious dishes suitable for every season and taste. Warming, low-calorie soups include Celeriac, Leek and Sage, and Mexican Bean; and there are high-fibre recipes such as Tagliatelle of Mussels, and Lamb Sweetbread Ravioli and, in the selection of warm salads, Scallops with Wild Strawberry Dressing, and Marinated Pigeon with Walnuts and Grapes. For a well-balanced meal, choose a starter that complements your main course in terms of both calorie, fibre and fat content as well as flavour.

Morels stuffed with Asparagus Mousse

1 × 140 g/5 oz breast of corn-fed chicken, skinned, boned and trimmed
12 asparagus spears
175 ml/6 fl oz/¾ cup natural, low-fat *fromage frais*
32 large morels, wiped
sea salt and freshly milled black pepper

Sauce
575 ml/1 pt/2½ cups chicken stock (see page 138)
1 dsp white wine
2 tomatoes, skinned, deseeded and diced (minced)
1 sprig cheril

Serves 4

Blend the chicken breast in a food processor or blender for 1 minute, then pass twice through a fine sieve. Cut the tips off the asparagus spears and put to one side. Trim off the woody ends and blanch the stalks until tender. Drain and refresh under cold running water, then squeeze out any excess liquid. Return the chicken breast mixture to the food processor or blender, add the asparagus stalks and blend for 1 minute. Pass through a fine sieve and chill.

Reserve 1 teaspoon of the *fromage frais* and beat the rest into the chilled chicken mixture. Season. Place in a piping bag fitted with a small nozzle and pipe into the morels. Heat the chicken stock to a gentle simmer and lower in the morels. Poach for about 5 minutes, and then add the asparagus tips to the liquid and simmer for a further 7 minutes. Remove the morels and the asparagus, drain and keep warm while preparing the sauce.

To make the sauce, add the white wine to the chicken stock and reduce over a high heat by two-thirds. Add the reserved teaspoon of *fromage frais* together with the diced tomato and the chervil and remove from the heat.

To serve, arrange 8 morels and 4 asparagus tips on each plate and surround with the sauce.

Fat: low Kcals: 133 Cholesterol: low Fibre: medium

Opposite, back left: *Galantine of Smoked Quail;* back right: *Chicken and Scallop Coulibiac;* front: *Morels Stuffed with Asparagus Mousse*

Galantine of Smoked Quail

2 rashers smoked lean back bacon,
fat and rind removed

115 g/4 oz tail fillet of veal

2 tbsp natural, low-fat *fromage frais*

1 egg white

1 clove garlic, skinned

55 g/2 oz/½ cup pistachio nuts,
shelled

½ green pepper, finely chopped

½ red pepper, finely chopped

2 truffles, peeled and finely
chopped

575 ml/20 fl oz/2½ cups chicken
stock (see page 138)

1 bunch thyme

4 small quail, boned

sea salt and freshly milled black
pepper

Sauce

50 ml/2 fl oz/¼ cup port

juice of 1 lemon

juice of 1 orange

2 tbsp clear honey

1 star anise

Garnish

115 g/4 oz/1 cup raspberries or
redcurrants

Serves 4

Preheat the oven to 220°C/425°F/gas 7.

Place the bacon, veal fillet, *fromage frais*, egg white, garlic clove and half the pistachio nuts in a food processor or blender and process until smooth. Press through a fine sieve into a clean bowl, then stir in the chopped peppers, truffles and the remaining pistachio nuts.

Bring the chicken stock to the boil in a saucepan with the thyme. Lay the boned quails skin-side down and pipe a quarter of the veal mousse onto each quail. Season with a little salt and pepper, then wrap the quail around the mousse to form the shape of the bird once more. Place the birds into an ovenproof dish and pour over the chicken stock. Cover and cook in the oven for 14 minutes until cooked through. When the quail are cooked, leave them to cool in the stock, then transfer to the refrigerator, still in the stock.

Meanwhile, to make the sauce, place all the ingredients together in a heavy-bottomed pan and reduce over a high heat for 8–10 minutes until the liquid resembles the consistency of thin jelly. Pass through a fine sieve.

To serve, slice each quail into 4 and place in the centre of each plate. Gently warm the sauce, pour it round the quail and garnish with the redcurrants or raspberries.

Fat: high Kcals: 322 Cholesterol: medium Fibre: low

Chicken and Scallop Coulibiac

300 ml/10 fl oz/1¼ cups chicken
stock (see page 138)

2 × 115 g/4 oz breasts of corn-fed
chicken, skinned, boned and
trimmed

2 scallops

115 g/4 oz large spinach leaves

6 sheets ready-made filo pastry

1 tbsp extra virgin olive oil

Bring the chicken stock to the boil in a pan, add the chicken breasts and poach for approximately 8 minutes until cooked through. Remove with a slotted spoon and place on a cooling tray.

Remove the scallops from the shells, cutting away any membrane and dark intestines, including the small curved muscle attached to the white meat. Wash and dry on kitchen paper. Remove the coral and reserve. Slice each piece of white meat in half and season.

In a separate pan, blanch the spinach in boiling water for 30 seconds, drain and refresh.

55 g/2 oz/¼ cup cooked wild and
    brown rice, mixed
sea salt and freshly milled black
    pepper

Sauce
2 shallots, roughly chopped
2 whole tomatoes
1 small potato, peeled and roughly
    chopped
1 bunch tarragon, roughly chopped
1 clove garlic, finely diced (minced)
1 dsp brandy
150 ml/5 fl oz/⅔ cup fish stock (see
    page 138)
1 pinch chilli pepper
juice of 1 lime

Serves 4

Preheat the oven to 180°C/350°F/gas 4.

To make each filo parcel, brush 3 sheets of pastry with a little olive oil and place one sheet on top of the other to form 3 layers. Place half the cooked rice on the top layer in the centre and season to taste with salt and freshly ground pepper.

Wrap a cooked cold chicken breast in half the blanched spinach leaves and place on top of the rice. Lay 2 pieces of scallop neatly on top of the spinach-wrapped chicken, then gather up the corners of the filo to encase the filling and twist to seal. Repeat as before with the remaining ingredients to form another parcel. Place on a greased baking sheet, and brush the tops with a little more olive oil. Bake in the oven for 12 minutes until golden brown. Remove from the oven and leave to rest for 5 minutes.

While the parcels are cooking, make the sauce. Heat a little olive oil in a pan and sweat the scallops, tomatoes, potato, tarragon and garlic for 2 minutes until the onion is translucent. Add the scallop corals and the brandy, ignite, then pour in the fish stock. Simmer for 15 minutes, then liquidize in a liquidizer or food processor and press through a fine sieve. Season with chilli pepper and lime juice. Keep in a warm place.

To serve, cut each parcel into 4 slices and place 2 slices each in the centre of 4 warm plates. Pour over a little sauce and serve immediately.

Fat: medium Kcals: 209 Cholesterol: high Fibre: low

Chickpea, Olive and Garlic Soup

170 g/6 oz/1 cup chickpeas
1 large onion, finely chopped
½ stick celery, finely chopped
4 large cloves garlic, diced (minced)
1 l/1¾ pt/4½ cups vegetable stock
    (see page 139)
1 bay leaf
1 sprig thyme
50 ml/2 fl oz/¼ cup extra virgin
    olive oil
sea salt and freshly milled white
    pepper
15 black olives, stoned and diced
    (minced)

Serves 4

Soak the chickpeas overnight, discard the soaking water, then cover with fresh water in a pan and bring to a rapid boil then simmer for approximately 1 hour until tender. Leave to cool, drain and remove the outer husks by rubbing them with a cloth.

Sweat the chopped onion, celery and garlic until soft in a covered pan. Add the vegetable stock, chickpeas, bay leaf and thyme, and simmer for 10 minutes. Blend the soup well, slowly adding the olive oil, in a food processor or blender, and then pass through a coarse sieve. Add the black olives as a garnish to finish the soup.

Fat: high Kcals: 194 Cholesterol: low Fibre: low

Carrot, Scallop and Coriander Soup

8 large king scallops

1 dsp extra virgin olive oil

6 medium-sized carrots, roughly
     chopped

1 large onion, roughly chopped

¼ stick celery, roughly chopped

½ clove garlic, diced (minced)

2 tsp coriander seeds, crushed

25 g/1 oz/¼ cup red lentils

1 bay leaf

1 l/1 pt 15 fl oz/4⅓ cups fish stock
     (see page 138)

1 bunch fresh coriander

sea salt and freshly milled black
     pepper

Serves 4

Remove the scallops from the shells, cutting away any membrane and dark intestines, including the small curved muscle from the white meat. Wash and dry on kitchen paper.

Heat the oil in a heavy-based saucepan, then sweat the carrots, onion, celery, garlic and crushed coriander until the onion is translucent. Carefully pick over the lentils to remove any stones. Add the lentils, bay leaf and 4 scallops, each one sliced into thirds. Pour over the fish stock and bring to the boil; cover the pan, reduce the heat and simmer for 10 minutes. Cut the stalks from the coriander (keep the leaves for garnishing), add to the pan and simmer, covered, for a further 10 minutes. Remove the soup from the heat and allow to cool slightly.

Liquidize the soup in a liquidizer or food processor, then pass through a fine sieve. Season to taste. Gently reheat the soup.

Fry the remaining 4 scallops in a hot non-stick frying pan (skillet) for 30 seconds on each side.

Place a scallop in the centre of each soup bowl, pour over the soup and garnish with coriander leaves. Serve immediately.

Fat: low Kcals: 175 Cholesterol: high Fibre: medium

Avocado and Sweetcorn Soup

1 small onion, finely chopped

1 clove garlic, diced (minced)

200 g/7 oz sweetcorn kernels,
     frozen or canned

2 green overripe avocados, peeled
     and stoned

1 tbsp light soy sauce

550 ml/20 fl oz/2½ cups chicken
     stock (see page 138)

1 tbsp natural, low-fat *fromage frais*

juice of ½ lemon

sea salt

cayenne pepper

Serves 8

In a non-stick saucepan, sweat the onion, garlic and 150 g/5 oz of the sweetcorn until the onion is translucent. Mash the avocado with a fork and add to the pan together with the soy sauce and chicken stock. Bring to the boil and simmer, uncovered, for 20 minutes. Remove from the heat and blend the soup in a food processor or blender. Pass through a fine sieve into a clean pan. Add the remaining sweetcorn, bring to the boil, then remove from the heat. Stir in the *fromage frais* and lemon juice, and season to taste with salt and cayenne pepper. Serve immediately with warm wholemeal bread.

Fat: medium Kcals: 88 Cholesterol: low Fibre: low

Previous page, left: *Carrot, Scallop and Coriander Soup;* right: *Chickpea, Olive and Garlic Soup*

Mexican Bean Soup

85 g/3 oz/½ cup dried kidney
beans, soaked overnight
4 large tomatoes, chopped
2 celery sticks, chopped
1 medium-sized onion, chopped
55 g/2 oz/⅓ cup dried butter
beans, soaked overnight
1 clove garlic, finely diced (minced)
1 small red chilli, deseeded
1 tsp fresh ginger, peeled and
roughly chopped
850 ml/1½ pt/3¾ cups water
150 ml/5 fl oz/⅔ cup tomato juice
2 tsp paprika
1 tbsp fresh parsley, chopped

Serves 4

Bring a pan of water to the boil and add the kidney beans. Bring to the boil again for at least 10 minutes. At the same time, bring another pan of water to the boil, add the butter beans and cook in the same way.

Drain the beans and place in a pan with the vegetables and all the other ingredients, except for the paprika and parsley. Bring to the boil and cook for 10 minutes, skimming the surface regularly. Cover and simmer for 1½ hours until the beans are tender.

Remove the chilli pepper and liquidize the soup in a food processor or blender and then pass through a fine sieve. Pour in the tomato juice and reheat gently. Season to taste.

To serve, ladle into individual soup bowls and sprinkle with a little paprika and the chopped parsley.

Fat: low Kcals: 156 Cholesterol: low Fibre: high

Mange-Tout, Mint and Caviar Soup

1 large Spanish onion, chopped
1 clove garlic, roughly chopped
225 g/8 oz/1½ cups leek, roughly
chopped
115 g/4 oz/¾ cup dried butter
beans, soaked overnight
1.5 l/50 fl oz/6¼ cups chicken
stock (see page 138)
1 bay leaf
1 sprig thyme
225 g/8 oz/1½ cups mange-tout
(sugar snap peas)
1 bunch mint
1 tbsp natural, low-fat *fromage frais*
1 tbsp caviar or fish roe
sea salt and freshly milled black
pepper

Serves 4

Preheat the oven to 180°C/350°F/gas 4.

In a covered, ovenproof pan sweat the onion, garlic and leek until the onion is translucent. Add the butter beans, chicken stock, bay leaf and thyme, boil for at least 10 minutes, and transfer to the oven. Cook for 40 minutes until the beans are tender. Remove from the oven and add the mange-tout (sugar snap peas) and the mint, reserving 4 small sprigs for the garnish. Boil on top of the stove for 5 minutes, then blend in a food processor or blender until smooth. Pass through a fine sieve and check for seasoning.

Serve in individual soup bowls with a swirl of *fromage frais* and a quarter of the caviar or fish roe in each bowl. Decorate with the mint sprigs and serve immediately.

Fat: low Kcals: 169 Cholesterol: low Fibre: high

Celeriac, Leek and Sage Soup; opposite: Mange-Tout, Mint and Caviar Soup

Celeriac, Leek and Sage Soup

1 large head celeriac

1 medium-sized onion

2 large leeks

1 tsp extra virgin olive oil

½ clove garlic, finely chopped

1 l/1¾ pt/4½ cups chicken stock (see page 138)

1 bay leaf

1 bunch sage

sea salt and freshly milled black pepper

Serves 4

Chop the celeriac, onion and leeks into rough squares and set aside a third of a leek for garnishing. Heat the oil in a pan and sweat the vegetables with the garlic until soft. Add the chicken stock, bay leaf and sage; bring to the boil and simmer, covered, for 20 minutes.

Cut the reserved leek into fine strips and blanch in salted water. Blend the soup in a food processor or liquidizer and press through a fine sieve. Season to taste and serve with the blanched leek strips on top.

Fat: low Kcals: 85 Cholesterol: low Fibre: medium

Parsnip and Chestnut Soup

450 g/1 lb parsnips, peeled and
    roughly chopped
1 Spanish onion, roughly chopped
½ clove garlic
1 bay leaf
140 g/5 oz/1 cup chestnuts,
    roasted and peeled
1.5 l/2½ pints/6¼ cups veal stock
    (see page 139)
4 tbsp natural, low-fat yoghurt (see
    page 142)

Garnish
2 sprigs parsley, finely chopped

Serves 4

Place the parsnips, onion, garlic, bay leaf, chestnuts and veal stock in a thick-bottomed pan and bring to the boil. Simmer for 40 minutes, skimming the surface regularly to remove any scum.

Blend the soup in a food processor or liquidizer and pass through a fine sieve into a soup terrine.

Stir in the yoghurt, sprinkle with the chopped parsley and serve immediately.

Fat: high Kcals: 169 Cholesterol: low Fibre: high

Marinated Red Mullet with Pressed Leek Terrine

4 × 85 g/3 oz fillets of red mullet,
    boned
900 g/2 lb baby leeks
1 small yellow pepper
3 tbsp extra virgin olive oil
1 tsp raw cane sugar
8 rocket leaves
12 oakleaf lettuce leaves
sea salt and freshly milled black
    pepper

Marinade
1 clove garlic, roughly chopped
1 tsp walnut oil
8 white peppercorns
8 sprigs parsley
1 shallot, sliced
1 bay leaf
1 lime
2 tbsp dry white wine
8 coriander seeds, crushed

Serves 4

Mix all the marinade ingredients together. Place the red mullet fillets in a shallow dish and spoon over the marinade. Leave to marinate for 2 hours in the refrigerator.

Line 4 small pâté terrines with cling film or plastic wrap. Wash the leeks and trim to fit the length of the terrines. Blanch for 2 minutes in lightly salted water, refresh under cold running water, drain and squeeze out the excess water. Lay in the terrines, season with black pepper, cover with cling film or plastic wrap and press with a heavy weight or dish filled with cold water in the refrigerator for at least 4 hours. At the end of this time, turn out the leeks onto an inverted dish and slice into 5 cm/2 in slices. Wrap in plastic again and return to the refrigerator.

Liquidize the yellow pepper with the olive oil and sugar in a liquidizer or food processor and pass through a fine sieve. Drain the red mullet fillets and cook, skin-side up, under a hot grill for 1½ minutes. Arrange on a plate on a bed of the salad leaves. Pour on the pepper sauce and grind over some freshly milled black pepper.

Fat: high Kcals: 252 Cholesterol: high Fibre: medium

Potato and Parsley Soup

3 large potatoes, roughly chopped

1 onion, roughly chopped

1 clove garlic, diced (minced)

1 stick celery, roughly chopped

1 bay leaf

1 bunch parsley

1.5 l/2½ pt/6¼ cups chicken stock
(see page 138)

sea salt and freshly milled black
pepper

Serves 4

In a thick-bottomed pan sweat the potatoes, onion, garlic, celery, bay leaf and parsley stalks for 5 minutes. Add the chicken stock and boil for 20 minutes. Add the parsley heads and cook for 5 minutes, then liquidize in a food processor or blender and pass through a fine sieve. Season with salt and pepper to taste and reheat before serving.

Fat: low Kcals: 122 Cholesterol: low Fibre: high

A Salad of Marinated Pigeon with Walnuts and Grapes

2 squab pigeons

55 g/2 oz/½ cup walnut pieces

140 ml/5 fl oz/⅔ cup red wine
vinegar

selection of salad leaves (e.g. lollo,
rocket, radicchio, spider endive)

115 g/4 oz/1 cup green seedless
grapes

Sauce

3 tbsp balsamic vinegar

1 dsp clear honey

1 tbsp walnut oil

Marinade

1 clove garlic, crushed

4 juniper berries, crushed

4 sprigs parsley

6 black peppercorns

140 ml/5 fl oz/⅔ cup balsamic
vinegar

140 ml/5 fl oz/⅔ cup red wine

1 tsp walnut oil

1 pinch salt

1 bay leaf

Serves 4

Preheat oven to 220°C/425°F/gas 7.

Mix all the marinade ingredients together. Place the squab pigeon, cut in half down the breast bone, in a shallow dish and spoon over the marinade. Leave in the refrigerator for 3 hours, then drain.

Whisk together all ingredients for the sauce in a bowl.

Roast the pigeons in the oven for 8-10 minutes until pink. Leave to rest for 5 minutes in a small dish, catching the cooking juices to add to the sauce later. Slice the pigeon breasts and arrange on top of the detached leg in the centre of the plate. Place the walnuts in a saucepan and bring to the boil in the red wine vinegar for 3 minutes.

Arrange the salad leaves around the plate with the grapes and walnuts. Gently heat the sauce and pour over the pigeon and salad.

Fat: high Kcals: 386 Cholesterol: low Fibre: low

Above, left: *Lamb Sweetbread Ravioli; above, right: Tagliatelle of Mussels;* opposite, back: *Brill and Crab Soufflé;* opposite, front: *Marinated Red Mullet with Pressed Leek Terrine*

Brill and Crab Soufflé

wholemeal and wholewheat flour

270 g/9 oz raw tomato concasse (see page 137)

55 g/2 oz white crab meat, finely diced (minced)

3 tsp lobster roe

115 g/4 oz fillet of brill, skinned

110 g/4 oz brown crab meat

1 egg yolk

2 tbsp natural, low-fat *fromage frais*

15 ml/½ fl oz/3 tbsp white wine

pinch cayenne pepper

3 egg whites

sea salt and freshly milled black pepper

Serves 4

Preheat the oven to 190°C/375°F/gas 5.

Grease 4 ramekins, then dust lightly with an equal mixture of wholemeal and wholewheat flour.

Mix the tomato concasse with the diced (minced) white crab meat and place a little of the mixture in the base of each ramekin. Grind a generous sprinkling of black pepper onto each, then place some lobster roe on top.

In a food processor or blender, blend the brill fillet, brown crab meat, egg yolk, *fromage frais*, white wine and cayenne pepper and process until smooth. Pass through a fine sieve and season to taste.

Whisk the egg whites until stiff and gently fold into the fish mousse. Spoon the mousse into the ramekins and smooth the tops with a flat knife. Bake in the oven for 12 minutes until golden brown and risen. Serve immediately.

Fat: medium Kcals: 158 Cholesterol: high Fibre: low

Tagliatelle of Mussels

350 g/12 oz saffron pasta (see
    page 141)

1 tsp extra virgin olive oil

1 tsp white wine vinegar

2 leeks, cut into 1 cm/½ in dice

55 g/2 oz/⅓ cup each of carrot,
    onion, celery and fennel, roughly
    chopped

1 sprig thyme

4 sprigs parsley

6 white peppercorns

1 bay leaf

75 ml/3 fl oz/⅓ cup dry white wine

900 g/2 lb mussels, scrubbed and
    bearded

150 ml/5 fl oz/⅔ cup natural, low-
    fat *fromage frais*

juice of ½ lemon

sea salt and freshly milled white
    pepper

Garnish

4 sprigs chervil

Serves 4

Roll out the pasta as thinly as possible, either by machine or by hand, and cut into tagliatelle strips, 1 cm/½ in wide.

Heat the olive oil in a frying pan (skillet), add the leeks and the vinegar and fry until the leek is a pale golden colour. Keep in a warm place.

In a large covered pan sweat the vegetables and thyme for 2 minutes. Add the parsley, peppercorns, bay leaf and white wine and reduce over a high heat by half. Add the mussels, cover once again and cook for 4 minutes until all the shells are open, shaking the pan from time to time so that the mussels cook evenly. Remove the mussels from their shells and keep warm. Drain the cooking liquor into a separate pan and reduce over a high heat by half. Once the liquor has reduced, stir in the *fromage frais*, lightly season, return the mussels to the sauce and warm gently; do not allow to boil.

Meanwhile, bring a large pan of lightly salted water to the boil, add a little lemon juice and drop in the pasta. Cook for 2–3 minutes until *al dente*, then drain.

Pile a quarter of the pasta in the centre of each plate, and pour over the sauce and mussels. Arrange the leeks around the plate, garnish with chervil and serve immediately.

Fat: medium Kcals: 446 Cholesterol: low Fibre: high

Lamb Sweetbread Ravioli

225 g/8 oz lamb sweetbreads

100 g/4 oz fresh wholemeal pasta
    (see page 140)

100 g/4 oz fresh wholemeal spinach
    pasta (see page 141)

1 × 140 g/5 oz breast of corn-fed
    chicken, skinned, boned and
    trimmed

1 clove garlic

1 egg white

2 tbsp natural, low-fat *fromage frais*

32 baby leeks, cut into 7.5 cm/3 in
    pieces

1 tsp olive oil

To clean the sweetbreads, soak them in cold water for 2 hours, then use a sharp knife to cut away any discoloured parts.

To make the sauce, place the shallots, chilli and herbs in a saucepan with the cider vinegar. Bring to the boil and leave to boil until the vinegar has reduced by two-thirds. Set to one side.

Preheat the oven to 205°C/400°F/gas 6.

Roll out both pastas, either by machine or by hand into 30 cm/12 in strips. Leave to rest for 20 minutes before rolling once again on the last pasta machine setting with the green and white pastas alternating in stripes to give a colourful sheet of dough.

To blanch the sweetbreads, place them in a saucepan, cover with fresh cold water, bring to the boil and simmer, uncovered, for 4 minutes. Drain, and when cool enough to handle, pull away the connecting ducts, then remove the skin and outer pieces of membrane.

sea salt and freshly milled black
    pepper
20 leaves spinach, blanched

Sauce
1 shallot, finely chopped
¼ fresh red or green chilli, finely
    chopped, deseeded
4 basil leaves, finely chopped
2 sage leaves, finely chopped
2 tbsp cider vinegar
1 tbsp natural, low-fat yoghurt (see
    page 142)
1 tsp clear honey
2 tbsp natural, low-fat *fromage frais*
1 egg white
2 tbsp extra virgin olive oil
salt and freshly milled black pepper

Garnish
1 bunch chervil

Serves 4

Meanwhile, place the chicken breast in a saucepan, just cover with lightly salted water, and bring to the boil. Cover the pan, turn down the heat and poach for 5 minutes. Drain, and when cool enough to handle, remove any remaining fat. Roughly chop up.

Roast the garlic clove, skin on, for 5 minutes in a hot oven, then rinse under cold water. Remove the skin then blanch the clove 3 times in boiling water.

Put the sweetbreads, chicken and garlic clove in a blender or food processor and blend to a smooth paste. Add the egg white and *fromage frais* to the mixture in the blender and blend again briefly. Pass the mixture through a fine sieve into a bowl and season to taste.

Lay out the strips of pasta on a clean flat surface; paint the pasta lightly with water. Place the filling mixture in a piping bag fitted with a plain 1 cm/½ in nozzle and pipe small mounds of filling, each mound approximately 5 cm/2 in in diameter, onto the pasta, spacing them evenly, just over 2.5 cm/1 in apart. When a strip is completed, place another piece of pasta over the top. Seal the layers by pressing between the mounds with your fingers. With a 7.5 cm/3 in pastry cutter, cut between the mounds into ravioli pieces, crimp up the edges with your fingers. Each strip should yield 8 pieces. Continue until all the filling has been used up. Bring about 2 litres/3½ pints of lightly salted water to the boil. Add the ravioli and cook for 3½ minutes, stirring from time to time until *al dente*.

Meanwhile, lightly season the leek pieces, brush with olive oil and cook under a medium grill for 3-4 minutes until lightly browned. Keep warm in a covered dish.

To finish the sauce, place the vinegar mixture in a *bain marie*. Whisk in the yoghurt, honey, *fromage frais*, oil and egg white until the mixture is of pouring consistency. Season to taste.

Serve the ravioli on large plates on a bed of spinach with the grilled leeks to one side, and garnished with chervil leaves.

Fat: high Kcals: 452 Cholesterol: high Fibre: high

A Warm Salad of Scallops with Wild Strawberry Dressing

selection of salad leaves (e.g. rocket, endive, radicchio, corn salad)

12 king scallops

juice of 1 lemon

sea salt and freshly milled white pepper

Tear the salad leaves into 1 cm/½ in pieces, wash them, shake any excess water from the leaves and place in 4 × 7.5 cm/3 in circular pastry cutters in the centre of the plate to form a neat selection of salad. Place in the refrigerator.

Set aside 20 strawberries for garnishing and purée the rest with the balsamic vinegar and olive oil in a food processor or blender to form a thick sauce, then pass through a fine sieve or muslin cloth.

Opposite: *A Warm Salad of Scallops with Warm Strawberry Dressing;* above: *A Salad of Marinated Pigeon with Walnuts and Grapes*

Dressing

225 g/8 oz/2 cups wild strawberries

2 tbsp balsamic vinegar

50 ml/2 fl oz/¼ cup extra virgin
   olive oil

Garnish

3 leeks

1 tbsp extra virgin olive oil

Serves 4

Remove the scallops from the shells, cutting away any membrane and dark intestines, including the small curved muscle attached to the white meat. Wash the flesh and dry on kitchen paper. Remove and discard the coral and cut each piece of white meat in half. Season lightly with salt, pepper and lemon juice. Heat a non-stick pan over a high heat, add the scallops and cook for 20-30 seconds on each side. When cooked, divide the pieces into 4 portions and arrange on top of the salad leaves. For the garnish, discard the dark green leaves of the leeks and cut the white parts into fine strips. Heat the oil in a frying pan (skillet) and fry the leek strips for 1 minute until golden brown.

Remove the cutters and pour the strawberry dressing into a small pan and warm slightly. Pour around the scallops and a little over the salad leaves. Sprinkle with the leek strips and serve immediately.

Fat: high Kcals: 278 Cholesterol: high Fibre: low

Scallop, Bacon and Mushroom Salad with Maple Dressing

500 g/1 lb 2 oz spinach

3 small rashers lean back bacon, fat and rind removed

1 pinch ground nutmeg

8 king scallops

sea salt and freshly milled black pepper

Dressing

2 shallots, finely chopped

1 tomato, skinned, deseeded and chopped

1 tbsp maple syrup

115 g/4 oz small chanterelle mushrooms

1 tsp walnut oil

2 tbsp white wine

Serves 4

Remove and discard the stalks from the spinach, blanch the leaves in boiling water for 30 seconds, drain and refresh. In a non-stick pan, fry the strips of bacon for approximately 3-4 minutes, until golden brown. Add the blanched spinach, season with the nutmeg and salt and pepper, and cook for 3-4 minutes. Press the spinach into 4 × 5 cm/2 in round pastry cutters and place one in the centre of each of 4 large plates. Remove the cutter leaving the moulded spinach on the plate. Keep in a warm place.

Remove the scallops from the shell, cutting away any membrane and dark intestines, including the small curved muscle from the white meat. Wash briefly and dry on kitchen paper. Cut each scallop into 3, then fry over a high heat in a clean non-stick pan for 20 seconds on each side. Place on top of the circles of spinach and keep warm.

To make the dressing, in the same pan fry the chopped shallots over a high heat in a non-stick pan until translucent. Add all the other ingredients and bring to the boil. Take off the heat, pour the warm dressing over the scallops and spinach and serve immediately.

Fat: high Kcals: 231 Cholesterol: high Fibre: medium

Mushroom and Tarragon Soup

450 g/1 lb flat mushrooms

1 bay leaf

1 large onion

1 clove garlic, crushed

2 sticks celery, roughly chopped

50 ml/2 fl oz/¼ cup white wine

1 tsp clear honey

2 tsp white wine vinegar

850 ml/1½ pt/3¾ cups vegetable stock (see page 139)

1 large potato, roughly chopped

1 bunch tarragon, finely chopped

300 ml/10 fl oz/1¼ cups skimmed milk

sea salt and freshly milled white pepper

Serves 4

Sweat the mushrooms, bay leaf, onion, garlic and celery in a deep pan over a low heat for 5 minutes. Add the white wine, honey, white wine vinegar, vegetable stock, potato and three-quarters of the tarragon, and simmer for 30 minutes.

Add the milk and liquidize in a food processor or blender with the remaining tarragon until smooth, then pass through a fine sieve. Season with salt and white pepper and reheat before serving.

Fat: low Kcals: 87 Cholesterol: low Fibre: high

Mushroom Ragout with Grilled Polenta

2 bay leaves

225 g/8 oz/1½ cups polenta

450 g/1 lb wild mushrooms, roughly
    chopped

1 tbsp sherry vinegar

8 cloves garlic, roasted

32 shallots, roasted and roughly
    chopped

4 tbsp cooked tomato concasse

6 sun-dried tomatoes, finely
    chopped

3 tbsp parsley, finely chopped

1 bunch asparagus tips, blanched

sea salt and freshly milled black
    pepper

Serves 4

Add the bay leaves to 450 ml/¾ pint/2 cups water and bring to the boil. Mix in the polenta and simmer for 15 minutes, stirring constantly. Pour into a shallow bowl and leave to cool. When cool and firm spread on a clean, flat surface and cut into rounds using a 5 cm/2 in circular pastry cutter.

Season with salt and pepper and cook under a hot grill for 3 minutes until lightly browned.

In a non-stick pan, sweat the wild mushrooms over a low heat for 4 minutes. Add the sherry vinegar, increase the heat and reduce for 1 minute. Stir in the garlic, shallots, tomato concasse and the sun-dried tomatoes and cook for 2 minutes. Add the parsley and asparagus tips to the mixture. Spoon over the grilled polenta rounds and serve immediately.

Fat: high Kcals: 316 Cholesterol: low Fibre: high

Fish and seafood

are high in protein and low in calories, and make wonderfully creative meals in any season. There is now a tremendous variety of fresh fish available in shops and supermarkets, ranging from red mullet and fresh tuna to salmon, sea bass and gurnard.

Turbot Steamed with Baby Spinach, Red Wine and Thyme

4 × 140 g/5 oz fillets of turbot,
  skinned
450 g/1 lb baby spinach, washed
1 pinch nutmeg
sea salt and freshly milled white
  pepper

Sauce
8 shallots, finely chopped
250 ml/8 fl oz/1 cup red wine
1 sprig thyme
300 ml/10 fl oz/1¼ cups fish stock
  (see page 138)

Serves 4

Preheat the oven to 205°C/400°F/gas 6.

Place the shallots, red wine and half the thyme in a pan and cook over a high heat until the shallots have absorbed all the wine. Add the fish stock and reduce by two-thirds.

Place the turbot on a steaming tray and steam over a pan of boiling water for 45 minutes.

Just before the end of the steaming time, sweat the spinach in a covered pan over a high heat for 3 minutes. Drain and season with a pinch of nutmeg, salt and white pepper. Season the wine sauce, remove the thyme and reserve for a garnish, if liked.

To serve, put a quarter of the spinach in the centre of the plate, place a turbot fillet on top and pour round the sauce.

Fat: medium Kcals: 277 Cholesterol: high Fibre: low

Opposite, from back: *Grilled Fillet of Mackerel with Apple Chutney, Gurnard Roasted with Garlic and Rosemary with Gazpacho and Turbot Steamed with Baby Spinach, Red Wine and Thyme*

Gurnard Roasted with Garlic and Rosemary with Gazpacho

4 × 225 g/8 oz gurnard, cleaned
   and gutted
4 cloves garlic, skinned
4 sprigs rosemary
juice of 1 lemon
sea salt and freshly milled black
   pepper

Sauce
1 red pepper
1 green pepper
1 yellow pepper
½ cucumber
8 tomatoes, skinned and deseeded
3 tbsp extra virgin olive oil
1 tbsp wholemeal soft breadcrumbs
1 clove garlic, finely diced (minced)
2 shallots, roughly chopped
1 tbsp balsamic vinegar
1 tsp honey
juice of ½ orange
sea salt and freshly milled white
   pepper

Garnish
20 cloves garlic, skinned
1 tsp olive oil
1 tsp maple syrup

Serves 4

Preheat the oven to 220°C/425°F/gas 7.

To make the garnish, peel the garlic cloves and blanch for 1 minute, drain and blanch 4 more times, using fresh water each time. Heat a roasting tray on top of the stove until smoking, then add the olive oil and syrup and brown the garlic cloves.

Stuff the cavities of each gurnard with a garlic clove and a sprig of rosemary, then trickle over a little lemon juice. Lightly season with salt and black pepper. Place on top of the garlic in the roasting tray and roast in the oven for 15–20 minutes until cooked through.

Meanwhile, make the sauce. Cut open each pepper, discard the seeds and cut the flesh into 3 mm/⅛ in dice; reserve half of each diced pepper for garnishing. Cut the cucumber in half and reserve 1 half for garnish. Cut the other half into small dice and liquidize with all the ingredients in a food processor or blender until puréed. Heat gently in a small pan.

To serve, spoon a pool of sauce onto the centre of each plate. Place a gurnard on top and garnish with diced pepper, cucumber slices and the roasted garlic.

Fat: high Kcals: 330 Cholesterol: high Fibre: medium

Grilled Fillet of Mackerel with Apple Chutney

4 tsp wholemeal flour

1 pinch cayenne pepper

1 sprig thyme

4 × 225 g/8 oz mackerel, filleted
    and boned

1 tbsp extra virgin olive oil

Apple chutney

1 small onion, finely chopped

1 pinch ground cumin

1 pinch ground ginger

1 pinch turmeric

1 pinch chilli pepper

1 clove garlic, finely diced (minced)

225 g/8 oz cooking apples, peeled
    and roughly chopped

2 tbsp sultanas

2 tbsp cider vinegar

2 tbsp clear honey

1 tsp hazelnut oil

Garnish

2 limes, cut into wedges

Serves 4

Season the flour with the cayenne pepper and thyme, then roll the mackerel fillets in the flour. Shake off any excess flour, lightly brush each fillet with olive oil and place on a grilling tray.

To make the chutney, sweat the onion with all the spices and garlic in a stainless steel pan for 2 minutes over a medium heat. Add the apples to the pan together with the rest of the chutney ingredients, and stew over a low heat for 25 minutes.

Grill the mackerel fillets under a hot grill for 8 minutes until golden brown. Serve with the warm chutney and a wedge of lime.

Fat: high Kcals: 472 Cholesterol: high Fibre: low

Salmon Baked with Samphire and Morels

4 × 110 g/4 oz fillets of salmon

2 shallots, finely chopped

1 sprig thyme

100 ml/4 fl oz/½ cup dry white wine

150 ml/5 fl oz/⅔ cup fish stock (see page 138)

170 g/6 oz samphire

285 g/10 oz/2 cups fresh morels, wiped

juice of 1 lime

2 tsp *crème fraîche*

25 g/1 oz/⅛ cup polyunsaturated spread

1 bunch chives, chopped

sea salt and freshly milled black pepper

Serves 4

Preheat the oven to 230°C/450°F/gas 8.

Heat a non-stick ovenproof pan on top of the stove over a high heat. Lightly season the pan with salt and pepper then add the salmon and cook for 30 seconds on each side. The presentation side of each fillet should now be face up. Place the pan in the oven for 8 minutes until the salmon is cooked through. Remove from the oven and place the salmon fillets on kitchen paper to drain.

In a non-stick saucepan cook the chopped shallots and the sprig of thyme until the shallots are translucent. Add the white wine and reduce over a high heat by two-thirds. Stir in the fish stock and reduce by a quarter.

In a separate non-stick pan gently cook the samphire and morels with the lime juice and a little black pepper for 3 minutes.

Remove the sauce from the stove and shake in the *crème fraîche* and the polyunsaturated spread off the heat. Season to taste and pass through a fine sieve into a warm sauce boat and stir in the chives.

Spoon a pool of sauce onto each plate, add a pile of samphire and place a salmon fillet on top with the morels arranged around the fish.

Fat: high Kcals: 297 Cholesterol: high Fibre: low

Opposite, from back: *Salmon Baked with Samphire and Morels;* above: *Cod Baked with Wild Mushrooms and Tarragon*

Cod Baked with Wild Mushrooms, Tarragon and White Wine

4 × 140 g/5 oz fillets of cod,
    skinned
115 g/4 oz wild mushrooms,
    preferably horn of plenty, wiped
1 small onion, chopped
1 bunch tarragon
100 ml/4 fl oz/½ cup white wine
115 g/4 oz/½ cup puy lentils, boiled
sea salt and freshly milled black
    pepper

Sauce
1 medium-sized carrot, finely
    chopped
4 shallots, finely chopped
2 sprigs tarragon
6 black peppercorns
1 star anise
250 ml/8 fl oz/1 cup white wine
575 ml/1 pt/2½ cups fish stock (see
    page 138)
85 g/3 oz/½ cup dried wild
    mushrooms

Serves 4

Preheat the oven to 190°C/375°F/gas 5. Put a baking sheet in the oven.

Place the cod fillets, wild mushrooms and chopped onion into an ovenproof dish with a lid. Add half the tarragon leaves (keeping the stalks for later) and cover with white wine. Season with sea salt and freshly ground black pepper. Place in the refrigerator until ready to cook.

Soak the dried mushrooms in warm water for 30 minutes, then drain. To make the sauce, in a non-stick saucepan brown the vegetables with the tarragon stalks, black peppercorns and star anise. When brown, add the white wine and reduce over a high heat by two-thirds. Add the fish stock and reduce again by two-thirds.

When the sauce has reduced, cook the cod fillets. Place the dish on the baking sheet in the oven and bake for approximately 10 minutes. Gently warm the puy lentils in a saucepan.

To serve, spoon a quarter of the lentils into the centre of each plate, place a cod fillet on top and arrange the wild mushrooms around. Check the sauce for seasoning, then pour over and garnish with the reserved tarragon.

Fat: low Kcals: 221 Cholesterol: high Fibre: low

Sea Bass Grilled with Sorrel and Chives

4 × 140 g/5 oz fillets of sea bass,
    scaled and boned
1 tbsp extra virgin olive oil
juice of 1 lemon
300 ml/10 fl oz/1¼ cups fish stock
    (see page 138)
1 tbsp dry vermouth
8 tbsp natural, low-fat yoghurt (see
    page 142)
1 bunch sorrel, stalks removed and
    chopped
1 bunch chives, finely chopped
salt and freshly milled white pepper

Serves 4

Brush the sea bass fillets with the olive oil and squeeze the lemon juice on top. Season with salt and white pepper. Refrigerate.

Add the vermouth to the fish stock and reduce over a high heat until it is of coating consistency. Leave to cool slightly and shake in the yoghurt. Keep warm in a *bain marie* on top of the stove.

Place the fish over hot charcoal or under a hot grill, skin-side down, and cook for 2 minutes. Carefully turn the fish and cook for approximately 3 minutes.

Meanwhile, in a separate non-stick pan, sweat the sorrel for 1 minute. To serve, place a quarter of the sorrel in the centre of each plate and put a sea bass fillet on top. Stir the chives into the sauce, check for seasoning and pour around the fish and sorrel.

Fat: medium Kcals: 194 Cholesterol: high Fibre: low

Red Snapper Cooked on a Bed of Aubergines with Lemon Vinaigrette

2 small aubergines (eggplants),
    cut into 6 mm/¼ in slices
2 lemons, roughly chopped
4 dsp extra virgin olive oil
2 tbsp white wine vinegar
1 tsp clear honey
4 × 110 g/4 oz red snapper fillets,
    scaled and boned
sea salt and freshly milled black
    pepper

Marinade
2 cloves garlic, crushed
10 black peppercorns, crushed
1 tbsp hazelnut oil
juice of ½ lemon

Garnish
1 bunch purple basil

Serves 4

Preheat the oven to 205°C/400°F/gas 6.

In a shallow dish, mix together the ingredients for the marinade together with a pinch of salt, and add the aubergine (eggplant) slices, turning to coat well. Cover and refrigerate for 1 hour.

In a liquidizer or food processor blend the chopped lemons, olive oil, vinegar and honey until smooth. Pass through a fine sieve into a small pan and put to one side.

Remove the aubergines (eggplants) from the marinade, place on a baking sheet and put the fish on top, skin-side up. Place in the oven and bake for 12 minutes until the fish is cooked through.

Drain the aubergines (eggplants) on kitchen paper, season with black pepper and arrange around one side of each plate. Warm the sauce through, taking care not to boil, and spoon a little onto the opposite side of the plate from the aubergines (eggplants). Place a fish fillet on top of the sauce and garnish with purple basil leaves.

Fat: high Kcals: 400 Cholesterol: high Fibre: low

Brill with Noodles and Clams

300 ml/10 fl oz/1¼ cups fish stock
(see page 138)

juice of 4 limes

1 star anise

450 g/16 oz clams

4 × 115 g/4 oz fillets of brill

225 g/8 oz saffron pasta (see
page 141)

juice of ½ lemon

2 shallots, finely chopped

45 g/1½ oz/¼ cup polyunsaturated
spread

1 tbsp natural, low-fat *fromage frais*

2 tbsp raw tomato concasse (see
page 137)

sea salt and freshly milled white
pepper

Serves 4

Simmer the fish stock, lime juice and star anise for 10 minutes. Pick over the clams and scrub them clean. Place in a steaming compartment over the fish stock and steam for 4 minutes. Keep warm, discarding any shells that have not opened.

Poach the brill fillets in the fish stock for 3½ minutes, then drain and keep warm, reserving the fish stock.

Meanwhile, cook the noodles in a large pan filled with lightly salted boiling water to which the lemon juice has been added, 3-4 minutes.

Place the shallots in the fish stock and reduce over a high heat by two-thirds. Off the heat, shake in the cold polyunsaturated spread and the *fromage frais*. Season to taste, then press through a fine sieve.

Arrange a brill fillet, a quarter of the noodles, clams and concasse on each plate. Pour the sauce around and garnish with a sprig of chervil.

Fat: high Kcals: 510 Cholesterol: high Fibre: medium

Scallops poached in Caraway and Saffron

12 king scallops

1 shallot, finely chopped

300 ml/10 fl oz/1¼ cups fish stock
(see page 138)

1 tbsp caraway seeds, crushed

2 tbsp white wine

2 courgettes (zucchini), cut into
strips

1 pinch saffron threads

45 g/1½ oz/¼ cup polyunsaturated
spread

2 tsps raw tomato concasse (see
page 137)

Garnish

4 springs cheril

Serves 4

Remove the scallops from the shell, cutting away any membrane and dark intestines, including the small curved muscle from the white meat. Remove and discard the corals. Wash and dry on kitchen paper. Slice each scallop into 4.

Place the shallot, fish stock, caraway seeds and white wine in a pan and reduce over a high heat by two-thirds. Add the scallops, cover and gently poach for 1 minute. Remove from the liquid and keep warm.

Quickly stir-fry the courgette (zucchini) strips and arrange in the centre of each plate.

Reduce the sauce over a high heat by half and then shake in the saffron and polyunsaturated spread.

To serve, arrange the scallops around the courgette (zucchini) strips and pour a little sauce around the scallops, garnish with the tomato concasse and a sprig of chervil.

Fat: high Kcals: 228 Cholesterol: high Fibre: low

Opposite, from top: *Sea Bass Grilled with Sorrel and Chives, Red Snapper Cooked on a Bed of Aubergines with Lemon Vinaigrette, and Brill with Noodles and Clams*

Red Mullet with Salad Niçoise

2 shallots, finely chopped

75 g/2½ oz/⅓ cup mange-tout
(sugar snap peas), blanched and
sliced

10 black olives, stoned and
chopped

4 large tomatoes, skinned,
deseeded and finely chopped

1 tbsp extra virgin olive oil

2 small potatoes

4 × 225 g/8 oz fillets of red mullet,
scaled

juice of ½ lime

sea salt and freshly milled black
pepper

Sauce

2 tbsp cider vinegar

1 pinch saffron powder

1 tbsp extra virgin olive oil

Serves 4

To prepare the salad, mix the shallots, mange-tout (sugar snap peas), olives and two-thirds of the diced tomato in a large bowl with the olive oil and lightly season. Peel the potatoes and cut into 6 mm/¼ in dice. Boil until cooked, about 15 minutes. Allow to cool and add the potatoes to the vegetable mixture.

To make the sauce, reduce the cider vinegar and saffron over a high heat by two-thirds and stir in the olive oil.

Season the red mullet fillets with the lime juice and some black pepper and grill, skin-side up, for 4 minutes.

To serve, place a quarter of the salad niçoise in the centre of each plate, top with a red mullet fillet and pour a little sauce over the fish. Garnish with the remaining diced tomato.

Fat: high Kcals: 323 Cholesterol: high Fibre: low

Parrot Fish Cooked in an Envelope

1 tsp walnut oil

4 sprigs parsley

4 × 40 g/5 oz fillets of parrot fish,
scaled, skin on

2 shallots, sliced

1 carrot, sliced

1 pinch fenugreek

4 star anise

8 black peppercorns

4 sun-dried tomatoes, roughly
chopped

50 ml/2 fl oz/¼ cup dry vermouth

juice of 1 lime

sea salt and freshly milled black
pepper

Serves 4

Preheat the oven to 220°C/425°F/gas 7.

Cut 4 squares of aluminium foil about 30 cm (12 in) square and fold each one in half to form a triangle. Open the foil out again to reform the square. Lightly oil one half of the foil squares and add one sprig of parsley and season with a little salt and pepper.

Place a fillet on top of each foil square and sprinkle with the shallots, carrot, spices, peppercorns and sun-dried tomatoes. Pour a little vermouth and lime juice over each fillet and fold the foil over to reform a triangle. Fold the edges double on each half to seal, fold over and seal the ends and place the packets on a baking sheet.

Bake in the oven for 8 minutes until cooked through. Serve immediately, opening the envelope at the table to enjoy the aroma as well as the flavour.

Fat: high Kcals: 236 Cholesterol: high Fibre: medium

Layers of Cabbage, Salmon and Pike Mousse with Scampi Tails

900 g/2 lb pike, filleted, boned,
  skinned and roughly chopped

3 tbsp natural, low-fat, *fromage
  frais*

1 egg white

juice of ½ lemon

1 pinch cayenne pepper

1 pinch celery salt

285 g/10 oz Savoy cabbage

900 g/2 lb side of salmon

2 shallots

75 ml/3 fl oz/⅓ cup dry white wine

150 ml/5 fl oz/⅔ cup fish stock (see
  page 138)

12 scampi tails, raw, peeled and cut
  in half lengthways

½ bunch tarragon

3 tbsp *crème fraîche*

6 tomatoes

1 bunch basil

2 tbsp extra virgin olive oil

1 tsp white wine vinegar

sea salt and freshly milled black
  pepper

Garnish

1 bunch chervil

Serves 4

Preheat oven to 180°C/350°F/gas 4.

To make the mousse, blend the pike, *fromage frais*, egg white, lemon juice, cayenne pepper and celery salt in a food processor or blender until smooth, then press through a fine sieve.

Using a 7.5 cm/3 in pastry cutter, cut 8 circles from the cabbage leaves. Blanch in lightly salted boiling water for 2 minutes, then re-fresh under running cold water.

Carefully cut the salmon through half its thickness lengthways. Use the pastry cutter to cut 8 circles out of the salmon, using a sharp knife around the outside edge of the cutter if necessary, and season. Cover 4 circles of the salmon with a cabbage circle and spread each with an eighth of the pike mousse. Place another layer of cabbage on top of the mousse, then follow with another layer of pike mousse and top with a circle of salmon. Place on a non-stick baking sheet and refrigerate until ready to cook.

Sweat the shallots in a covered non-stick pan until translucent. Add the white wine and reduce over a high heat by two-thirds. Pour in the fish stock, and reduce again by half. Bring to a gentle simmer, add the scampi tails and tarragon leaves and cook for 1½ minutes. Remove the scampi from the stock, drain and keep warm. Shake the *crème fraîche* into the stock, off the heat, and pass into a sauce boat and keep warm.

Dice (mince) one tomato and liquidize the rest of tomatoes together with the basil, olive oil and white wine vinegar in a liquidizer or food processor until smooth, then pass through a fine sieve. Warm slightly in a pan, and add just before serving. Put the salmon in the oven for 18 minutes. Remove from the oven and place in the middle of each plate and spoon both sauces around the salmon. Spoon the green sauce around the salmon, then the circle of red sauce along the edge of a green sauce. Circle the sauce with 6 scampi tails. Garnish with chervil on top of each tail.

Fat: high Kcals: 587 Cholesterol: high Fibre: medium

Grilled Tuna with Black-eyed Beans and Coriander

100 g/4 oz/1 cup black-eyed beans

2 tsp coriander seeds, crushed

2 cloves garlic, diced (minced)

1 bunch coriander, chopped

juice of 2 limes

2 tbsp extra virgin olive oil

4 × 150 g/5 oz tuna steaks, skinned and boned

1 small onion, finely chopped

4 tbsp cooked tomato concasse (see page 136)

150 ml/5 fl oz/⅔ cup tomato vinaigrette (see page 138)

sea salt and freshly milled black pepper

Serves 4

Soak the black-eyed beans in water overnight.

Make a marinade by combining the crushed coriander seeds, the garlic and a quarter of the chopped coriander in the lime juice and 1 tablespoon of the oil. Place the tuna steaks in a shallow dish and spoon over the marinade. Leave to marinate in a cool place for 2 hours.

Meanwhile, discard the soaking water from the black-eyed beans, rinse and cover with fresh cold water, lightly salted, in a non-stick saucepan. Simmer, covered, for 1 hour or until the beans are tender. Drain and reserve.

Heat the remaining oil in a large frying pan (skillet), add the onion and sweat until translucent. Stir in the tomato concasse and remove from the heat. Add the black-eyed beans, tomato vinaigrette and the rest of the chopped coriander.

Remove the fish steaks and reserve the marinade. Season the steaks, then grill, preferably over charcoal, cooking for 4 minutes on each side; brush the steaks with marinade while cooking. Warm the bean and tomato mixture, make a small mound in the centre of each plate and serve with a tuna steak placed on top.

Fat: high Kcals: 359 Cholesterol: high Fibre: medium

Opposite: *Layers of Cabbage, Salmon and Pike Mousse with Scampi Tails;* above: *Grilled Tuna with Black-eyed Beans*

Salmon Poached in Champagne served with Cucumber and Watercress Salad

4 tbsp dry champagne
4 × 110 g/4 oz fillets of salmon,
    skinned

Salad
4 tbsp natural, low-fat yoghurt (see
    page 142)
1 tsp parsley, chopped
1 tsp fresh mint, chopped
1 tsp clear honey
1 red apple, grated
1 small cucumber, cut into 4 cm/
    1½ in batons
1 bunch watercress, stalks removed
sea salt and freshly milled black
    pepper

Garnish
4 wedges lime

Serves 4

Bring the champagne to the boil in a shallow pan. Add the salmon and cook for 4 minutes the over a high heat. Remove from the heat and leave to cool in the champagne. Chill in the refrigerator.

To prepare the salad, mix the yoghurt, parsley, mint and honey together and season with salt and pepper. Pour over the grated apple, cucumber and watercress leaves just before serving and toss well.

To serve, place a quarter of the salad on each plate and rest a cold salmon fillet on top. Add a wedge of lime. This is delicious with a cold new potato salad.

Fat: high Kcals: 272 Cholesterol: high Fibre: low

Trout Wrapped in Chinese Leaves with Ginger and Spring Onion

4 Chinese leaves

4 × 225 g/8 oz fillets of trout, skinned

½ clove garlic, crushed

1 tsp fresh ginger, grated

2 bunches spring onions (scallions), cut into short lengths

1 piece lemon grass, cut into 4 lengthways

sea salt and freshly milled black pepper

Sauce

2 shallots, finely chopped

2 tbsp dry sherry

3 tsp light soy sauce

150 ml/5 fl oz/⅔ cup fish stock (see page 138)

juice of 1 lemon

1 pinch five spice powder

Serves 4

Blanch the Chinese leaves in boiling water for 30 seconds and refresh under cold water. Season the fish with salt and pepper, and add the garlic and the ginger. Fold the fillets into 3 and wrap in the blanched Chinese leaves.

Put the spring onions (scallions), lemon grass and wrapped fish into a bamboo steamer, and steam, covered, for 12 minutes.

To make the sauce, place the shallots, sherry and soy sauce into a non-stick pan and reduce over a high heat until all the liquid has been absorbed by the shallots. Add the fish stock, lemon juice and the five spice powder and stir well.

To serve, arrange the onions and strips of lemon grass around the fish and spoon over the sauce.

Fat: high Kcals: 243 Cholesterol: high Fibre: medium

Meat, poultry and game

Meat, poultry and game are extremely versatile and play an important part in a balanced diet, being an excellent source of protein. Choose from traditional roasted meats such as Venison roasted with Pistachio Mousse, Cabbage and Juniper, and Roasted Fillet of Pork with Apricot, and Onion to more exotic dishes served with fruit and vegetables. These include Duck Breast roasted with Lentils and Kumquat Marmalade and Barbecued Chicken Chilli and Pineapple wrapped in a Cornflour Pasty.

Duck Liver Mousse with Sprouting Lentils and Smoked Bacon

1 medium-sized onion, finely chopped

1 garlic clove, diced (minced)

2 tbsp brandy

150 ml/5 fl oz/⅔ cup red wine

4 sheets ready-made filo pastry

1 tbsp extra virgin olive oil

1 tbsp wholemeal flour

1 × 115 g/4 oz breast of corn-fed chicken, skinned, boned and trimmed

1 egg yolk

350 g/¾ lb fresh duck livers

1 pinch celery salt

2 dsp natural, low-fat *fromage frais*

4 egg whites

4 rashers lean smoked back bacon, fat and rind removed, cut into lardons

240 g/8 oz/1 cup sprouting lentils

Garnish

1 bunch chervil

Serves 4

Preheat the oven to 180°C/350°F/gas 4. Sweat the onion and garlic in a pan until translucent. Add the brandy and red wine, and reduce to a syrup consistency; leave to cool.

Using a 12.5 cm/5 in pastry cutter, cut out 8 circles of filo pastry. Brush each one with a little olive oil and put half of the circles on top of the others to form 4 circles and place in a small, deep round tin. Bake in the oven for 5 minutes until golden brown, leave to set and remove from the tin.

Grease 4 ramekins and lightly dust with wholemeal flour. Finely chop the chicken breast and blend with the egg yolk, onion and brandy mixture, duck livers, celery salt and *fromage frais* in a food processor or blender until smooth. Pass through a fine sieve. Whisk the egg whites until stiff and fold into the mixture. Fill the greased ramekins with the mousse and level the tops with a flat knife. Place in an ovenproof tray filled with water and cook in the oven for 20 minutes.

Meanwhile, fry the bacon lardons in a non-stick pan over a high heat until golden brown. Add the sprouting lentils, lower the heat and cook for 1 minute.

Plunge the ramekins in hot water up to their rims for 30 seconds, and turn out into the filo baskets. Place in the centre of each plate and surround with the bacon and lentils. Garnish with chervil and serve.

Fat: high Kcals: 387 Cholesterol: high Fibre: low

Opposite, from back: Duck Liver Mousse with Sprouting Lentils and Smoked Bacon, Fillet of Beef with Mango Glaze, and Pheasant Stuffed with Truffle Mousse and Creamed Fennel

Pheasant Stuffed with Truffle Mousse and Creamed Fennel

2 pheasants, oven-ready

115 g/4 oz tail fillet of veal

2 × 115 g/4 oz breasts of corn-fed chicken, skinned, boned and trimmed

1 clove garlic, diced (minced)

2 tbsp natural, low-fat *fromage frais*

1 egg white

4 truffles, peeled and chopped

2 tsp pink peppercorns, crushed

575 ml/1 pt/2½ cups chicken stock (see page 138)

2 bulbs fennel

100 ml/4 fl oz/½ cup white wine

4 tbsp *crème fraîche*

1 quantity Champneys bechamel (see page 141)

1 tbsp olive oil

sea salt and freshly milled black pepper

Serves 4

Preheat the oven to 220°C/425°F/gas 7.

Separate the legs and thighs from the rest of the pheasant carcass. Remove the skin and trim the leg meat from the bones and chop it roughly. Extract the breast and thigh meat whole and slice down the centre to make a cavity for stuffing. Place the chopped leg meat, veal fillet, chicken breast, garlic, *fromage frais* and egg white in a food processor or blender and mix until smooth. Pass through a fine sieve and add the truffles and pink peppercorns. Stuff the breasts and thighs with this mixture, wrap in muslin and tie at the ends. Bring the chicken stock to the boil in a large pan and lower in the muslin-wrapped pheasant. Cover and simmer gently for 5 minutes.

Remove and reserve the tops from the fennel and finely chop the bulbs. Blanch the chopped bulbs in lightly salted water for 3 minutes, refresh under cold running water and drain.

Bring the white wine to the boil in a pan, reduce over a high heat by half then add the chopped fennel. Remove the sauce from the heat and stir in the *crème fraîche* and the bechamel.

Heat the olive oil in a roasting tray on the top of the stove. Remove the pheasant from the muslin and brown for 2 minutes in the hot tray. Transfer to the oven and roast for 5 minutes until cooked and golden brown.

Chop the reserved fennel tops and add to the sauce. Warm through but do not reboil. Remove the pheasant from the oven and cut the thighs into 6 mm/¼ in slices and arrange around the breasts. Serve with a little sauce and fennel fronds.

Fat: high Kcals: 457 Cholesterol: high Fibre: low

Fillet of Beef with Mango Glaze

4 × 110 g/4 oz fillet steaks of beef, trimmed

1 large, ripe mango

1 tsp peach and lemon chutney (see page 140)

575 ml/1 pt/2½ cups veal stock (see page 139)

2 shallots, finely chopped

50 ml/2 fl oz/¼ cup madeira

2 small carrots, roughly chopped

1 large onion, roughly chopped

1 clove garlic, finely diced (minced)

1 tsp mild curry powder

1 tsp sultanas

1 pinch powdered ginger

1 egg yolk

75 ml/3 fl oz/⅓ cup extra virgin olive oil

2 large leeks

3 tbsps raw tomato concasse (see page 137)

Serves 4

Preheat the oven to 205°C/400°F/gas 6.

Tie the beef fillets with string around the centre to ensure they keep their shape while cooking.

Peel the mango then cut in half. Cut half into strips 5 cm × 3 mm/2 in × ⅛ in; reserve for the garnish. Purée the other half of the mango in a food processor or blender. Stir in the peach and lemon chutney.

Bring the veal stock to the boil and reduce over a high heat until reduced by three-quarters.

Sweat the shallots in a covered non-stick pan over a low heat until translucent. Deglaze with the madeira, reduce over a high heat by half, then pour in the veal stock. In a separate pan sweat the carrots, onions, garlic, curry powder, sultanas and ginger in a covered non-stick pan for 5 minutes over a low heat. Cover with water and cook for 30 minutes. Add to the chutney and mango mixture.

Heat a roasting tray on the top of the stove, season the beef fillets and seal on both sides in the hot tray. Roast for 12 minutes.

Meanwhile, in a large bowl whisk the egg yolk with 1 tablespoon of warm water until light and frothy. Add to the chutney mixture and mix in well. Remove the beef from the oven and spoon a little of the mango glaze over each fillet. Place under a hot grill for approximately 45 seconds.

Heat the oil in a large pan until smoking, discard the green parts of the leeks and cut the white parts into thin strips and fry until golden brown. Drain on kitchen paper.

Add the reserved mango strips and the tomato concasse to the sauce and warm slightly. Spoon a pool of sauce onto each plate and place a glazed fillet on top. Garnish with the strips of leek.

Fat: high Kcals: 464 Cholesterol: high Fibre: medium

Stuffed Breast of Chicken with a Tomato Vinaigrette

4 × 140 g/5 oz breasts of corn-fed chicken, skinned, boned and trimmed

2 large carrots, peeled and grated

1 large leek, finely chopped

16 black olives, stoned and roughly chopped

575 ml/1 pt/2½ cups chicken stock (see page 138)

sea salt and freshly milled black pepper

Vinaigrette

3 large, ripe tomatoes

2 tbsp extra virgin olive oil

1 leaf basil

1 tbsp cider vinegar

Serves 4

Make a sharp incision about 2 cm/⅔ in long into one side of each chicken breast to form a pocket.

Season the grated carrot, chopped leek and the olives with salt and pepper and stuff the chicken breasts with the mixture. Overlap the pocket openings to seal the mixture inside.

Preheat the oven to 220°C/425°F/gas 7.

In an ovenproof dish, bring the chicken stock to the boil on the top of the stove and add the chicken breasts. Place in the oven for approximately 10 minutes until poached.

Meanwhile, liquidize all the ingredients for the vinaigrette in a food processor or blender and pass through a fine sieve.

When the chicken is cooked, slice each breast diagonally into 5 pieces and place on individual plates. Spoon round the vinaigrette and serve immediately.

Fat: high Kcals: 298 Cholesterol: high Fibre: low

Roasted Baby Pigeon with Coriander and Pearl Barley Dumplings

4 squab pigeons

1 bay leaf

2 cloves garlic, finely diced (minced)

1 small onion, finely chopped

150 ml/5 fl oz/⅔ cup red wine

3 tomatoes, roughly diced

700 ml/1¼ pt/3 cups chicken stock (see page 138)

1 bunch coriander

225 g/8 oz/1 cup pearl barley

1 × 115 g/4 oz breast of corn-fed chicken, skinned, boned and trimmed

2 fresh duck livers

2 tbsp natural, low-fat *fromage frais*

1 tsp extra virgin olive oil

1 tbsp maple syrup

Preheat the oven to 205°C/400°F/gas 6.

Remove the breasts from the pigeon carcasses and leave in a cool place. Trim the wing bones and knuckles and place the bones in a non-stick pan with the bay leaf, 1 clove of garlic and onion. Cook on a high heat for approximately 4-5 minutes until brown, then add the red wine and tomatoes, 575 ml/1 pint/2½ cups of the chicken stock and the stalks from the coriander, reserving the leaves for the dumplings. Reduce over a high heat by two-thirds, then pass through a fine sieve, discarding the bones.

In a separate pan, cook the pearl barley in boiling salted water for 20 minutes, then refresh under cold running water and drain.

Combine the chicken breast, duck liver, *fromage frais* and the remaining clove of garlic in a food processor or blender and blend until smooth. Pass through a sieve and add half the coriander leaves, chopped, and half the pearl barley. Mix well and form into 20 dumplings.

Heat the olive oil and the maple syrup in a roasting tray on the top of the stove. Add the peeled shallots and cook for 1 minute. Season the

Roasted Baby Pigeon with Coriander and Pearl Barley Dumplings

20 shallots, peeled

Garnish
4 sprigs chervil

Serves 4

pigeon breasts and add to roasting tray. Cook the leg and breast meat and shallots together in the oven for 15 minutes until golden brown.

Remove from the oven and keep the pigeon and shallots warm. Strain the excess fat from the pan and place on top of the stove on a low heat. Add the remaining pearl barley, the remaining chopped coriander leaves and the sauce; warm through for 3-4 minutes.

Meanwhile, bring the remaining chicken stock to the boil in a separate pan. Drop in the chicken dumplings and simmer, with the lid on, for 3 minutes until cooked through.

To serve, heap a quarter of the warmed pearl barley and coriander mixture in the centre of each plate and place a pigeon breast on top. Surround with 5 dumplings and 5 shallots and spoon a little sauce over to cover the plate.

Fat: high Kcals: 699 Cholesterol: high Fibre: low

Duck Breast Roasted with Lentils and Kumquat Marmalade

4 × 170 g/6 oz breasts of female
    Barbary duck
170 g/6 oz/1 cup puy lentils
sea salt and freshly milled black
    pepper

Marmalade

300 ml/10 fl oz/1¼ cups fresh
    orange juice
225 g/8 oz/2 cups kumquats,
    sliced

Sauce

3 shallots, finely chopped
50 ml/2 fl oz/¼ cup port
150 ml/5 fl oz/⅔ cup red grape
    juice
150 ml/5 fl oz/⅔ cup chicken stock
    (see page 138)
2 tsp arrowroot

Garnish

4 sprigs chervil

Serves 4

Preheat the oven to 205°C/400°F/gas 6.

Remove the skin and fat from the duck breasts, reserving the fat, and season. Replace the fat on top of each breast and place in a roasting tray. Boil the lentils in salted water for 15 minutes, then refresh under cold running water.

To make the marmalade, place the orange juice in a stainless steel pan and reduce over a high heat by two-thirds, add the kumquats and cook for 10 minutes over a medium heat.

To make the sauce, sweat the shallots in a non-stick pan until translucent. Add the port and the grape juice and reduce over a high heat until the liquid reaches syrup consistency. Mix the arrowroot with a little water to form a smooth paste then stir into the syrup to thicken, still on the heat.

Roast the duck breasts for 10 minutes in the oven until pink. Remove from the roasting tray and leave to rest for 5 minutes, then slice. Drain off the excess fat from the roasting tray, add the lentils, season with salt and pepper and warm over a low heat on the top of the stove.

Put a quarter of the warmed lentils in the centre of each plate, rest the duck breast slices on top and spoon over a little kumquat marmalade. Pour the sauce around the duck and garnish with chervil.

Fat: low Kcals: 301 Cholesterol: medium Fibre: medium

Grilled Corn-Fed Chicken with Walnut and Celeriac Cakes

1 large head celeriac, peeled

1 clove garlic, finely diced (minced)

1 small onion, finely chopped

2 rashers smoked lean back bacon,
    cut into lardons

2 dsp walnuts, crushed

30 g/1 oz/½ cup low-fat Cheddar
    cheese, grated

1 egg white

1 tbsp olive oil

4 × 140 g/5 oz breasts of corn-fed
    chicken

sea salt and freshly milled black
    pepper

Sauce

300 ml/10 fl oz/1¼ cup apple juice

150 ml/5 fl oz/⅔ cup chicken stock
    (see page 138)

1 cooking apple, grated

Serves 4

Preheat the oven to 220°C/425°F/gas 7.

Slice one quarter of the celeriac into thin, round slices and put to one side. Grate the rest of the celeriac and combine with the garlic, onion, bacon rashers and walnuts in a non-stick pan, put on a lid, and sweat for 5 minutes until slightly soft. Leave to cool. Add the grated cheese and egg white and mix in thoroughly. Season. Press a quarter of the mixture into a 7.5 cm/3 in circular pastry cutter onto a non-stick roasting tray, pushing down firmly with the back of the hand. Remove the cutter to leave a cake shape. Repeat 3 more times. Place in the oven and cook for 15 minutes until golden brown.

Place the celeriac slices on a grilling tray and dribble over the olive oil. Lightly season. Season the chicken breasts and place them skin-side down on top of the celeriac. Grill under a medium-hot grill for 4 minutes on one side, then turn over and cook for a further 5 minutes until cooked through.

To make the sauce, pour the apple juice and chicken stock into a stainless steel pan and reduce over a high heat by two-thirds. Add the grated apple and immediately remove from the heat.

To serve, place a cake in the centre of each plate, rest a chicken breast on top and pour a little sauce around. Drain the slices of celeriac on kitchen paper to remove any excess fat, and arrange around the plate for the garnish.

Fat: high Kcals: 382 Cholesterol: high Fibre: low

Overleaf, left: *Grilled Corn-Fed Chicken with Walnut and Celeriac Cakes;* right: *Duck Breast Roasted with Lentils and Kumquat Marmalade*

Roasted Fillet of Veal with Roasted Shallots and Garlic with a Madeira Sauce

2 cloves garlic
1 × 170 g/6 oz breast of corn-fed
  chicken, skinned, boned and
  trimmed
2 bunches watercress, stalks
  removed
2 tbsp natural, low-fat *fromage frais*
4 × 140 g/5 oz fillets of veal, larder
  trimmed and tied
1 piece caul fat
20 shallots, peeled
90 ml/3½ fl oz/⅓ cup madeira
300 ml/10 fl oz/1¼ cups reduced
  veal stock (see page 139)
sea salt and freshly milled black
  pepper

Garnish
4 sprigs chervil

Serves 4

Preheat the oven to 230°C/450°F/gas 8.

Roast the garlic, skins on, in the oven for 5 minutes, then rinse in cold water. Remove the skins, then blanch in boiling water three times. Turn the oven temperature down to 190°C/375°F/gas 5.

Combine the chicken and watercress in a food processor or blender, mix in the *fromage frais* lightly season, and process until a firm mousse is formed. Pass the mousse through a fine sieve.

Spread a layer of mousse on top of each veal fillet, then wrap each fillet in caul fat. Heat a non-stick ovenproof pan on the top of the stove, then add the veal fillets and seal for 2 minutes on each side. Remove from the pan with a slotted spoon and keep warm. Add the garlic and shallots to the pan and lightly brown. Return the veal fillets to the pan, then transfer to the oven for 15 minutes.

When the fillets are cooked, remove them from the pan together with the shallots and garlic and keep in a warm place. Place the pan on the top of the stove, deglaze the cooking juice with the madeira and reduce by half. Stir in the veal stock, reheat and season to taste.

Place a veal fillet on each plate, spoon over the sauce and surround with garlic cloves and shallots. Garnish with chervil leaves and serve immediately.

Fat: medium Kcals: 289 Cholesterol: high Fibre: low

Saddle of Venison Roasted with Pistachio Mousse, Cabbage and Juniper

450 g/1 lb saddle of venison loin

1 Savoy cabbage

1 onion, sliced

4 juniper berries

4 tbsp water

1 tbsp clear honey

1 tsp arrowroot, mixed with a little
water to form a paste

sea salt and freshly milled black
pepper

Mousse

2 × 140 g/5 oz breasts of corn-fed
chicken, skinned and boned

1 pinch celery salt

1 pinch cayenne pepper

2 tbsp natural, low-fat *fromage frais*

1 egg

45 g/1½ oz/¼ cup pistachio nuts,
shelled and roughly chopped

Herb crust

4 tbsp fresh wholemeal
breadcrumbs

1 clove garlic, finely diced (minced)

2 tbsp fresh mixed herbs (e.g.
tarragon, chervil, basil), chopped

Sauce

1.35 kg/3 lb venison bones

2 carrots

1 leek

2 sticks celery

2 onions

2.25 l/4 pt/10½ cups cold water

3 sprigs thyme

1 bay leaf

150 ml/5 fl oz/⅔ cup red wine

50 ml/2 fl oz/¼ cup port

450 g/1 lb/4 cups gooseberries or
cranberries

Serves 4

Preheat the oven to 205°C/400°F/gas 6.

To make the sauce, place the bones and vegetables on a roasting tray and brown in the oven for 25–30 minutes. Remove from the oven and place in a pan with the cold water. Add the thyme and the bay leaf. Bring to the boil, skim the surface of the water to remove any excess fat, reduce the heat slightly and simmer for 2 hours.

Pass this stock through a fine sieve into a clean pan, discarding the bones. Reserve the thyme and add the red wine, port and gooseberries or cranberries. Reduce over a high heat by three-quarters and pass through a fine sieve once again.

To make the pistachio mousse, place the chicken breast, celery salt, cayenne pepper, *fromage frais* and the egg into a food processor or blender and mix till smooth. Pass through a fine sieve. Add the pistachios and spread a thin layer over the length of the saddle of venison.

To make the herb crust, blend the breadcrumbs, garlic and herbs in a food processor or blender till well mixed. Press onto the chicken mousse. Place the saddle of venison on top of the thyme in a roasting tray and roast for 20 minutes until cooked but still pink.

Meanwhile, shred the cabbage and add to a large pan with the onion and juniper berries. Add the water and lightly season. Cover and steam over a high heat for approximately 10 minutes until the cabbage is tender. Drain off any excess liquid.

Remove the gooseberries or cranberries from the sauce using a slotted spoon and put into a pan with the honey. Heat gently and keep in a warm place.

Serve the venison cut into 2.5 cm/1 in slices on a little of the cabbage, with the sauce around the outside, garnished with the warmed fruit.

Fat: high Kcals: 533 Cholesterol: high Fibre: high

Roasted Quail Stuffed with Chervil Mousse

1 × 140 g/5 oz breast of corn-fed
   chicken, skinned, boned and
   trimmed

1 egg

115 g/4 oz natural, low-fat *fromage
   frais*

1 bunch chervil, chopped

4 quails, boned (reserve the bones
   for the sauce)

2 rashers lean back bacon, fat and
   rind removed

8 baby carrots

8 baby courgettes (zucchini)

8 baby leeks

8 baby beetroot (beet)

8 shallots

8 mange-tout (sugar snap peas)

Chutney

450 g/1 lb swede, roughly diced
   (minced)

2 medium-sized onions, chopped

55 g/2 oz/¼ cup sultanas

2 tomatoes, roughly chopped

2 tbsp cider vinegar

1 cooking apple, diced (minced)

Sauce

4 shallots, finely chopped

10 button mushrooms

50 ml/2 fl oz/¼ cup white wine

300 ml/10 fl oz/1¼ cup chicken
   stock (see page 138)

6 sprigs chervil

1 bay leaf

2 black peppercorns, crushed

Serves 4

To make the chutney, cook the swede in a little water until tender, drain and mash until smooth. Sweat the chopped onions, sultanas and tomatoes in a covered non-stick pan until the onion becomes translucent. Add the cider vinegar and reduce over a high heat by half. Mix in the apple and the swede and lightly season.

To make the sauce brown the quail bones in a small, deep pan. Sweat the shallots and mushrooms in a covered non-stick pan until the shallots have softened. Add the white wine to the pan and reduce over a high heat by half. Add the chicken stock, quail bones, chervil, bay leaf and peppercorns and simmer for 20 minutes.

Preheat the oven to 205°C/400°F/gas 6.

Process the chicken breast in a food processor or blender for 2 minutes, add the egg and season, then pass through a sieve. Return the mixture to the processor or blender and beat in the *fromage frais* and chopped chervil. Fill the quail cavities with the mousse. Place half a bacon rasher on each quail breast and put the quail in a non-stick roasting tray. Roast for 10 minutes until cooked through.

Meanwhile, cook the baby vegetables in lightly salted water, simmering for about 8–10 minutes until tender.

Spoon a quarter of the chutney into a circle in the centre of each plate, place a quail on top and surround with vegetables. Spoon over the sauce and serve.

Fat: high Kcals: 500 Cholesterol: high Fibre: high

Opposite, top: *Saddle of Venison Roasted with Pistachio Mousse, Cabbage and Juniper;* bottom: *Roasted Quail Stuffed with Chervil Mousse*

Smoked Gammon Brochettes

1 red pepper

1 green pepper

1 courgette (zucchini)

8 mushrooms

500 g/1 lb 2 oz smoked gammon,
    cut into 2.5 cm/1 in dice and
    soaked in cold water for 4 hours

1 bay leaf

1 head celeriac

2 cooking apples

55 g/2 oz smoked goat's cheese

1 tbsp extra virgin olive oil

1 small onion, finely chopped

1 clove garlic, finely diced (minced)

1 egg

juice of 1 lemon

Marinade

6 black peppercorns

1 tbsp sesame oil

1 pinch celery salt

1 pinch cayenne pepper

1 bunch coriander

50 ml/2 fl oz/¼ cup white wine

1 tbsp soy sauce

Serves 4

Mix together all the ingredients for the marinade. Chop the peppers, courgette (zucchini) and mushrooms into 2.5 cm/1 in squares and thread them onto 8 bamboo skewers with the smoked gammon and pieces of bay leaf. Place the skewers in a shallow dish, spoon over the marinade and leave in the refrigerator for 3 hours. Turn the skewers halfway through the marinading time.

Preheat the oven to 180°C/350°F/gas 4. Grease a baking sheet.

Grate the celeriac, apples and goat's cheese into a large bowl. Heat the olive oil and fry the onion and garlic in a frying pan (skillet) until translucent. Add to the celeriac and apple mixture and stir in well. Whisk the egg, lightly season and add to the grated mixture. Divide the mixture into 4 and push each portion into a 5 cm/2 in circular pastry cutter and push down firmly. Remove the cutters and bake for 25 minutes until golden brown.

Cook the brochettes for 8 minutes under a hot grill, turning the skewers halfway through the cooking time. Serve with freshly squeezed lemon juice.

Fat: high Kcals: 434 Cholesterol: high Fibre: medium

Quail with Sweet Pepper Sauce and Autumn Vegetables

1 × 170 g/6 oz breast of corn-fed
    chicken, skinned, boned and
    trimmed
1 red pepper, deseeded
1 pinch celery salt
1 pinch cayenne pepper
1 tbsp natural, low-fat *fromage frais*
2 tbsp white wine
4 quail, boned
4 rashers lean back bacon, fat and
    rind removed
selection of turned root vegetables,
    blanched and tossed in 1 tsp
    clear honey
sea salt and freshly milled black
    pepper

Sauce

2 shallots, finely chopped
½ red pepper, diced (minced)
juice of ½ lemon
300 ml/10 fl oz/1¼ cups chicken
    stock (see page 138)
1 tomato
1 tbsp extra virgin olive oil

Garnish

4 sprigs chervil

Serves 4

Preheat the oven to 180°C/350°F/gas 4.

Roughly chop the chicken breast and put in a food processor or blender with the red pepper, a pinch each of celery salt and cayenne pepper, the *fromage frais* and the white wine. Process until smooth then pass through a fine sieve to produce the sweet pepper forcemeat. Season the boned quail and stuff with the forcemeat. Place a piece of bacon on top of each bird as protection against drying out. Put in a roasting tray and cook in the oven for 17 minutes until the skin is crisp and golden.

Meanwhile, make the sauce. Sweat the chopped shallots and pepper in a covered non-stick pan until the shallots become translucent. Deglaze the pan with the lemon juice, add the chicken stock and reduce over a high heat by two-thirds. Liquidize the whole tomato with the olive oil in a liquidizer or blender and pass through a fine sieve.

When the quail are cooked, slice each one into 3 and place in the centre of each plate. Shake the tomato and olive oil mixture into the hot sauce and remove from the heat. Spoon the sauce around the quail and arrange the turned vegetables around the quail. Garnish with chervil sprigs.

Fat: high Kcals: 393 Cholesterol: medium Fibre: medium

Roasted Fillet of Pork with Apricot and Onion

4 small fillets of pork

75 g/3 oz/⅓ cup dried apricots

100 ml/4 fl oz/½ cup white wine

1 tbsp extra virgin olive oil

1 large onion, finely sliced

1 tbsp potato starch mixed with a
little water to form a paste

Marinade

4 tbsp light soy sauce

150 ml/5 fl oz/⅔ cup red wine

4 tbsp sake or dry sherry

1 tbsp clear honey

1 sprig fresh thyme, or a pinch dried
thyme

Garnish

2 carrots

Serves 4

Combine all the marinade ingredients. Remove all excess fat from the pork fillets, place in a shallow dish and spoon over the marinade. Leave in a cool place to marinate for 2 hours.

Preheat the oven to 180°C/350°F/gas 4.

Place the apricots in a pan with the white wine. Bring to the boil, cover the pan and continue to boil for 20–30 minutes until the apricots are soft.

Meanwhile, heat a little olive oil in a frying pan (skillet), add the onion and sweat until soft.

Drain and reserve the marinade from the pork. Heat a non-stick roasting tray on the top of the stove, then seal the fillets over a high heat until golden brown. Place in the oven and roast for 20 minutes until firm but moist.

Meanwhile, in a saucepan, blanch the carrots in lightly salted water. Remove, allow to cool, then cut into strips.

Chop up the softened apricots and add the onions. In a separate saucepan, bring the marinade to the boil. Stir in the potato starch paste to thicken, and cook for a further 2 minutes, stirring continuously.

When the pork is cooked, leave to rest for 5 minutes before cutting each fillet into slices 1 cm/½ in thick. Spoon a mound of apricot and onion mixture onto individual plates. Place the sliced fillets on top, pour a little of the marinade sauce over and garnish with carrot strips.

Fat: high Kcals: 247 Cholesterol: medium Fibre: low

Poached Fillet of Veal with Broccoli Mousse and Carrot Purée

1 × 140 g/5 oz fillets of veal,
trimmed of any fat and sinews

1 piece caul fat

1.75 l/3 pt/7½ cups veal stock (see
page 139)

2 shallots, finely chopped

2 tbsp balsamic vinegar

6 tbsp fresh orange juice

24 baby carrots

450 g/1 lb/2½ cups carrots, roughly
chopped

Mousse

2 tbsp natural, low fat *fromage frais*

To make the mousse, combine the *fromage frais*, chicken breast, egg white, broccoli florets and garlic in a food processor or blender. Lightly season, blend until smooth and pass through a fine sieve. Spread a quarter of the mousse into a dome shape on top of each veal fillet and wrap in caul fat.

Pour a third of the veal stock into a pan and reduce over a high heat by two thirds.

Sweat the shallots in a covered non-stick pan over a medium heat until translucent. Add the balsamic vinegar and 2 tablespoons of the orange juice; reduce over a high heat to syrup consistency. Add the reduced veal stock, bring to the boil and simmer for 5 minutes.

Blanch the baby carrots in a pan of lightly salted boiling water for 2 minutes. In a separate pan, reduce the remaining orange juice over a high heat by half, add the baby carrots and boil in the juice until cooked, about 12 minutes.

Poached Fillet of Veal with Broccoli Mousse and Carrot Purée

1 × 140 g/5 oz breast of corn-fed
  chicken, skinned, boned and
  trimmed
1 egg white
3 heads broccoli
1 clove garlic
sea salt and freshly milled black
  pepper

Serves 4

Season the remainder of the veal stock and bring to the boil. Lower in the veal fillets and simmer for 8 minutes until cooked.

Meanwhile, put the roughly chopped carrots in a separate pan, just cover with water and cook until tender. Purée in a food processor or blender.

To serve, place a quarter of the carrot purée in the centre of each plate and rest a veal fillet on top. Place the baby carrots around the purée and spoon over the sauce.

Fat: low Kcal: 205 Cholesterol: medium Fibre: medium

Marinated Fillet of Pork with Sweet Peppers

2 × 240 g/8 oz fillets of pork, fat removed

1 large green pepper, halved and deseeded

1 large yellow pepper, halved and deseeded

1 large red pepper, halved and deseeded

2 tbsp extra virgin olive oil

2 potatoes, cooked and roughly chopped

2 tbsp white wine vinegar

1 pinch chilli powder

fresh orange juice, to mix

1 tsp low-calorie granulated sweetener

1 tbsp linseeds

1 tsp sesame oil

sea salt and freshly milled black pepper

Marinade

1 stick cinnamon

2 tbsp soy sauce

2 cloves garlic, finely diced (minced)

1 tsp fresh ginger, peeled and grated

1 tbsp clear honey

1 pinch cayenne pepper

1 tsp coriander seeds, crushed

1 tsp sesame oil

Garnish

4 sprigs chervil

Serves 4

Mix all the marinade ingredients together. Place the pork fillets in a shallow dish, spoon over the marinade and leave to marinate in the refrigerator for 3 hours. Turn the fillets twice during this time.

Preheat the oven to 180°C/350°F/gas 4.

Towards the end of the marinading time, cut half of each pepper into 1 cm/½ in diamond shapes and reserve. Place each remaining pepper half separately into a liquidizer or food processor together with a third each of the olive oil, cooked potato and white wine vinegar; add a pinch of chilli powder to the red pepper mixture. Blend until smooth, then pass each sauce separately through a muslin cloth into individual bowls. Each sauce should be of the same consistency; if not, adjust with a little orange juice. Taste the sauces, and if too bitter sweeten with a little granulated sweetener, as the taste of peppers varies according to the time of year.

Heat a roasting tray, drain the meat from the marinade and sprinkle the fillets with linseeds. Seal the meat in the tray over a high heat and then roast in the oven for 18–20 minutes until golden brown.

Meanwhile, heat the pepper sauces separately. When the meat is cooked, leave to rest for 5 minutes. Heat the sesame oil in a pan and stir-fry the pepper diamonds over a very high heat for 1 minute. Cut the fillets into 6 mm/¼ in slices and divide equally between the plates, arranging them in the centre. Pour a quarter of each warmed sauce around the fillet. Sprinkle the pepper diamonds on top of the sauces and garnish the fillet with a sprig of chervil.

Fat: high Kcals: 365 Cholesterol: high Fibre: low

Veal Sweetbreads with Leeks and Watercress

150 ml/5 fl oz/⅔ cup veal stock
  (see page 139)
675 g/1½ lb veal sweetbreads
2 shallots, finely chopped
75 ml/3 fl oz/⅓ cup white wine
4 bunches watercress, leaves only
2 tbsp natural, low-fat *fromage frais*
4 tbsp/⅓ cup Champneys
  bechamel (see page 141)
2 tbsp clear honey
2 tbsp extra virgin olive oil
30 baby leeks, cut into 10 cm/4 in
  lengths
sea salt and freshly milled black
  pepper

Serves 4

Reduce the veal stock by four-fifths over a high heat. Add the sweetbreads and blanch for 8 minutes. Remove and place in a shallow dish and reserve the stock. Cover the sweetbreads with aluminium foil and press with a heavy weight or pan filled with cold water for 2 hours in the refrigerator.

To make the purée, sweat the shallots until translucent in a covered non-stick pan together with the white wine. Add the reserved stock and reduce by half over a high heat. Add the leaves from 2 bunches of watercress and purée in a food processor or blender until smooth. Season and pass through a sieve into a sauce boat.

Combine the *fromage frais* with the remaining watercress leaves, bechamel, 1 tablespoon of the honey and a little salt and pepper and mix in a food processor or blender until smooth.

Heat the olive oil in a small pan. Cut the sweetbreads into 8 rounds using a 4.5 cm/2 in circular pastry cutter, season and fry for 5 minutes until golden brown, turning once. Remove from the pan and keep warm. Add the remaining honey and 1 teaspoon of water to the pan and blanch the leeks for 3 minutes.

Pour a quarter of the wine and watercress sauce onto each plate. Sandwich a quarter of the blanched leeks between 2 sweetbread rounds and place to one side of the sauce. Serve with the watercress purée on top.

Fat: high Kcals: 429 Cholesterol: high Fibre: high

Overleaf, left: *Marinated Fillet of Pork with Sweet Peppers;* right: *Veal Sweetbreads with Leeks and Watercress*

Pheasant and Quail Stuffed with Apple and Cranberry Forcemeat

1 tbsp extra virgin olive oil

1 small onion, chopped

75 g/2½ oz veal, roughly diced

4 rashers lean smoked bacon, fat
    and rind removed

2 leaves sage, chopped

3 leaves basil, chopped

1 dash Worcester sauce

2 cooking apples, grated

55 g/2 oz/½ cup cranberries

1 pheasant, boned

1 quail, boned

1 clove garlic, finely diced (minced)

1 sprig of thyme

575 ml/1 pt/2½ cups chicken stock
    (see page 138)

sea salt and freshly milled black
    pepper

Serves 4

Preheat the oven to 220°C/425°F/gas 7.

Heat the olive oil in a pan, add the chopped onion, cover and sweat until translucent. Combine the onion with the veal, 2 rashers of bacon, sage, basil and a dash of Worcester sauce in a food processor or blender and blend until smooth. Transfer to a bowl, lightly season, then thoroughly mix in the grated apple and half the cranberries.

Place the pheasant between cling film or plastic wrap and lightly beat. Remove the plastic film. Repeat with the quail and lay on top of the pheasant.

Place the stuffing inside the 2 birds and roll to reform the shape of the birds. Place the remaining 2 rashers of bacon over the top of the birds and tie with string.

Spread the diced (minced) garlic on a roasting tray to form a bed for the birds and place them on top. Roast the birds in the oven for 40 minutes, basting every 10–15 minutes, until cooked; the breast should still be pink and juicy and the juices run clear when the flesh is pierced with a skewer.

When cooked, allow the birds to rest for 5–10 minutes. Meanwhile, strain the fat from the roasting tray, place the tray on top of the stove and add the thyme and the chicken stock. Reduce over a high heat by two-thirds.

Cut the birds into 6 mm/¼ in slices and arrange a quarter on each plate, together with the stuffing. Spoon over the sauce and serve.

Fat: high Kcals: 329 Cholesterol: medium Fibre: low

Barbecued Chicken Chilli and Pineapple Wrapped in a Cornflour Pasty

400 g/14 oz breast meat of corn-fed chicken, skinned, boned and trimmed

baby pineapple, skin and stalk removed, cut into chunks

¼ iceberg lettuce, finely sliced

30 g/1 oz/½ cup low-fat Cheddar cheese, grated

2 tomatoes, sliced

Marinade

1 tsp clear honey

1 fresh red or green chilli, deseeded and finely chopped

1 pinch paprika

juice of 1 lemon

1 dash Worcester sauce

1 clove garlic, crushed

Pasty dough

150 g/5½ oz/1¼ cups wholemeal flour

100 g/3½ oz/¾ cup cornflour or cornstarch

1 tsp paprika

approximately 100 ml/4 fl oz/½ cup cold water

sea salt and freshly milled black pepper

Serves 4

Cut the chicken breasts into 2 cm/¾ in cubes, or large enough so that they will not fall through the barbecue grill bars, and place in a shallow dish. Mix all the marinade ingredients together, then spoon over the cubes of chicken and leave to marinate in a cool place for 2 hours.

Meanwhile, make the pasty dough. Sift the wholemeal flour, corn-flour or cornstarch, paprika and salt and pepper to taste into a large mixing bowl, then stir round to mix the flours evenly. Make a well in the centre, then gradually pour in cold water, stirring continuously and drawing in flour to make a smooth ball of dough. Transfer the dough to a lightly floured surface and knead for 2 minutes. Divide the dough into 4 equal portions and place in the refrigerator for 20 minutes. On a lightly floured surface, roll out each portion of dough to a thickness of 3 mm/⅛ in and return to the refrigerator.

Grill the chicken pieces for 5 minutes over the barbecue until almost cooked. When the chicken is nearly ready, add the rolled pasty dough portions to the barbecue and cook for 1½ minutes on each side. Place a quarter of the chicken pieces in the centre of each pasty, then fold over the sides to enclose the filling, leaving the top open. Serve with chunks of pineapple, sliced iceberg lettuce, grated Cheddar cheese and slices of tomato.

Fat: medium Kcals: 388 Cholesterol: medium Fibre: medium

Vegetable dishes

Vegetable dishes provide new ideas for tasty main courses and help vegetarians obtain all the vitamins, minerals and protein necessary for a balanced diet. The exciting range of fresh vegetables now available can also be used to make delicious side dishes, always important in a meal. Fresh, uncooked foods are the healthiest of all; boost your intake of raw vegetables by mixing them with fruits, cheeses, grains, pulses and meats in a variety of irresistible salads.

Carrot and Peanut Terrine

675 g/1½ lb spinach, stalks removed

1 large courgette (zucchini)

85 g/3 oz/⅓ cup smooth peanut butter

1 tsp peanut oil

110 g/4 oz/1 cup peanuts, in husks

2 cloves garlic, finely diced (minced)

1 medium-sized Spanish onion, finely chopped

900 g/2 lb carrots, grated

1 red pepper

1 green pepper

1 yellow pepper

6 dsp orange and basil dressing (see page 137)

sea salt

Serves 14

Preheat the oven to 240°C/475°F/gas 9.

Put the spinach, 3 tablespoons of water and a little salt in a non-stick pan, cover with a lid, and sweat for 2–3 minutes until cooked. Refresh under cold running water and drain. Line a 1.1 litre/2 pint/5 cup terrine with greaseproof (wax) paper, then line with the spinach, making sure the spinach hangs well over the sides to cover the top later.

Blanch the courgette (zucchini) in boiling salted water for 1 minute, refresh under cold running water, drain and remove top and bottom parts. Spread with half of the peanut butter.

Heat the peanut oil in a large pan. Remove the peanuts from their husks, reserve a few for garnishing and sweat the rest over a low heat with the garlic, onion, carrot and remaining peanut butter, 5 minutes.

Place the peppers on a baking sheet and roast in the oven until the skins blister, 8–10 minutes. Place the peppers in sealed plastic bags for 5 minutes to loosen the skins. Remove the skins, cut each into 2 rough 5 cm/2 in squares and remove the seeds.

Divide the carrot and peanut mixture into 4, and press one quarter into the base of the spinach-lined terrine. Cover with half of the peppers, then add another layer of carrot and peanut mixture. Place the courgette (zucchini) in the centre of the terrine, followed by a layer of carrot and peanut mixture, then the remaining peppers. Top with the last quarter of carrot and peanut. Overlap the hanging spinach on top, press with a heavy weight and leave in the refrigerator until cold.

Invert the terrine onto a plate and shake hard to remove from the dish. To serve, cut the terrine into 2.5 cm/1 in slices and either reheat in a microwave for 1½ minutes or gently steam for 3 minutes. Place a few slices on each plate, spoon round a little warm orange and basil dressing and sprinkle over a few peanuts to garnish.

Fat: high Kcals: 429 Cholesterol: low Fibre: high

Bean and Pepper Lasagne

45 g/1½ oz/⅓ cup dried butter
  beans
45 g/1½ oz/⅓ cup dried black-eyed
  beans
45 g/1½ oz/⅓ cup dried red kidney
  beans
45 g/1½ oz/⅓ cup dried flageolet
  beans
1 red pepper
1 green pepper
1 yellow pepper
2 tbsp extra virgin olive oil
6 shallots, finely chopped
2 cloves garlic, finely diced (minced)
6 sun-dried tomatoes, roughly
  chopped
25 g/1 oz/¼ cup black olives
1 bunch basil, shredded
115 g/4 oz cooked spinach
1 pinch nutmeg
115 g/4 oz wholemeal pasta, thinly
  rolled (see page 140)
300 ml/10 fl oz/1¼ cups
  Champneys bechamel (see page
  141)
55 g/2 oz low-fat Cheddar cheese,
  grated
4 tbsp cooked tomato concasse
  (see page 138)
50 ml/2 fl oz/¼ cup white wine

Garnish
4 sprigs chervil

Serves 4

Soak all the beans in separate bowls overnight; remove any beans that float to the surface. Discard the soaking water and place the beans in separate pans, cover with fresh water and bring to the boil. Boil for 10 minutes, then reduce the heat, put on lids, and simmer until tender, between 1-2 hours. Refresh under cold running water, then leave to drain well.

Cut the peppers into 6 mm/¼ in dice. Heat the oil in a frying pan (skillet) and sweat the peppers, shallots, 1 garlic clove, the sun-dried tomatoes, olives and shredded basil until the shallots turn translucent. Reserve a few beans for garnishing and mix the rest with the contents of the pan.

Meanwhile, place the spinach, the remaining garlic clove, a pinch of nutmeg and 3 tablespoons of water in a pan and cook over a high heat for 2-3 minutes. Refresh under cold running water, drain and chop very finely.

Preheat the oven to 180°C/350°F/gas 4.

To assemble the lasagne, using a deep 7.5 cm/3 in pastry cutter cut 16 circles of pasta and blanch in boiling water for 1½ minutes. Refresh, then place 4 circles on a greased baking sheet. Replace a pastry cutter over each circle. Use half the spinach to cover each pasta circle and place a second circle on top. Make another layer of filling with half the bean and pepper mixture and cover with a pasta circle. Repeat the layers of spinach and bean and pepper mixture as before, finishing with a pasta circle on top. Make sure there is a gap of 6 mm/¼ in between the top of the pastry cutter and the last pasta circle.

Mix the bechamel and grated cheese together and pour into the cutters to fill. Bake in the oven for 20 minutes until bubbling and golden.

Meanwhile, warm the tomato concasse with the white wine. Transfer each pastry cutter to an individual plate, using a fish slice to aid you. Run a sharp knife around the inside edge of the pastry cutters and remove from the lasagne. Spoon round the tomato concasse and reserved beans and garnish with a sprig of chervil.

Note: This dish can also be made in a deep baking sheet using the same method. Use double quantities, and cut the pasta into strips approximately 5 cm/2 in wide to fit the width or length of the tray.

Fat: high Kcals: 449 Cholesterol: low Fibre: high

Leek and Herb Sausages with Pickled Cabbage

170 g/6 oz/2 cups fresh wholemeal
   breadcrumbs

1 pinch celery salt

1 pinch freshly milled black pepper

85 g/3 oz/1 cup low-fat Chedder
   cheese, grated

½ tsp coarse grain mustard

115 g/4 oz/1 cup wholemeal flour

1 egg white

55 g/2 oz/¾ cup fine dry
   breadcrumbs

2 tbsp extra virgin olive oil

sea salt

Pickled cabbage

½ large red cabbage, cut into 6
   mm/¼ in slices

300 ml/10 fl oz/1¼ cups red wine
   vinegar

1 tbsp pickling spice

2 tbsp clear honey

4 oz/115 g leeks, finely chopped

1 medium-sized onion, finely
   chopped

1 clove garlic, finely diced (minced)

2 tsp fresh basil, chopped

2 tsp fresh chervil, chopped

2 tsp fresh coriander leaves,
   chopped

Serves 4

Layer the cabbage with sea salt and leave for 4 hours. Boil the vinegar, pickling spice and honey for 5 minutes in a stainless steel saucepan. Wash the salt from the cabbage and pat the slices dry. Pour the hot vinegar mixture over the red cabbage and leave for 1 week in a sterilized pickling jar.

When the cabbage is ready, fry the leek, onion and garlic in a nonstick pan until golden brown, about 3 minutes. Add the chopped herbs and cook for another minute. Stir in the fresh breadcrumbs, celery salt, black pepper, Cheddar cheese and mustard and immediately remove from the heat. Allow to cool slightly then mould the mixture into sausage shapes and coat with the flour, egg white and finally the dry breadcrumbs.

Preheat the over to 180°C/350°F/gas 4.

Heat the olive oil in a frying pan (skillet), place the sausages in the oil and brown slightly. Remove from the pan and place on a baking sheet. Cook in the oven for 8 minutes until golden brown and then drain on kitchen paper.

Strain the vinegar from the pickled cabbage and place a mound in the centre of each plate; rest a sausage on top and serve immediately.

Fat: high Kcals: 402 Cholesterol: low Fibre: high

Lentil and Wild Mushroom Bolognese

Lentil and Wild Mushroom Bolognese

350 g/285 g/10 oz wholemeal pasta (see page 140)

2 dsp extra virgin olive oil

6 shallots, finely chopped

1 red pepper, finely diced

1 green pepper, finely diced

1 clove garlic, finely diced (minced)

170 g/6 oz wild mushrooms (e.g. girolles, morels), wiped

5 tbsp raw tomato concasse (see page 137)

55 g/2 oz/⅓ cup green lentils

55 g/2 oz/⅓ cup puy lentils

Roll out the pasta in a machine or by hand, then cut into tagliatelle.

To make the tomato sauce, sweat the onion, carrot, garlic, tomatoes, basil, parsley and bay leaf in a covered non-stick pan until the onions are translucent. Add the white wine and tomato purée and cook for 1 minute over a moderate heat. Pour in the vegetable stock, cover and gently simmer over a low heat for 20 minutes, then pass through a fine sieve and lightly season.

Heat 1 tablespoon of olive oil in a separate pan, add the shallots, peppers and garlic, cover and sweat for 2 minutes until the shallots are translucent. Add the wild mushrooms and cook for 3 minutes. Add the tomato concasse and cook for a further minute. Add half the tomato sauce to this mixture.

Meanwhile, cook the lentils in separate pans for 20 minutes each until soft. Drain and toss in the remaining olive oil.

sea salt and freshly milled black
   pepper

Sauce

1 onion, finely chopped

1 carrot, finely chopped

1 clove garlic, finely diced (minced)

5 tomatoes, roughly chopped

4 leaves fresh basil

4 sprigs parsley

1 bay leaf

75 ml/3 fl oz/⅓ cup dry white wine

1 tsp tomato purée

150 ml/5 fl oz/⅔ cup vegetable
   stock (see page 139)

Garnish

4 sprigs basil

Serves 4

Bring a large pan of lightly salted water to the boil and drop in the tagliatelle. Cook for 3 minutes until *al dente*.

To serve, pile a quarter of each of the lentils in one corner of each plate and place a quarter of the cooked tagliatelle to the side of the lentils. Spoon a quarter of the mushroom bolognese next to the tagliatelle and pour a little tomato sauce around. Garnish with a sprig of basil and grind over some black pepper.

Fat: medium Kcals: 475 Cholesterol: low Fibre: high

Aubergine Gâteau with Provençale Vegetables

Endive Salad with Balsamic Honey Dressing

2 heads of white Belgian endive

2 heads of red Belgian endive

4 peppers: 1 red, 1 yellow, 1 black,
  1 orange

1 tbsp olive oil

1 bunch spring onions (scallions),
  roughly chopped

45 g/1½ oz/⅓ cup whole almonds,
  lightly roasted

Dressing

1 dsp white wine vinegar

1 dsp clear honey

4 dsp balsamic vinegar

1 tsp extra virgin olive oil

sea salt and freshly milled black
  pepper

Serves 4

To make the dressing, warm the white wine vinegar in a small pan and dissolve the honey in it. Add the balsamic vinegar, whisk in the oil, and season with salt and pepper.

Arrange a quarter of the endive leaves on each plate. Cut the peppers into neat dices and sauté in a little olive oil; season. Sprinkle the spring onions (scallions), peppers and the almonds onto the leaves, distributing them evenly between the plates, then sprinkle with a little of the dressing and serve.

Fat: high Kcals: 196 Cholesterol: low Fibre: medium

Salad of Smoked Salmon, Quail's Eggs and Samphire

12 quail's eggs

115 g/4 oz/¾ cup samphire

1 red oakleaf lettuce

1 head curly endive

225 g/8 oz smoked salmon

juice of 1 lime

Dressing

zest and juice of 2 lemons

½ tsp English mustard

1 egg yolk

9 dsp extra virgin olive oil

Garnish

borage flowers

4 sprigs of chervil

Serves 4

To make the dressing, place the lemon zest and juice, mustard and egg yolk in a food processor or blender and mix well. With the machine still turned on add the oil in a steady stream then pass the mixture through a muslin cloth. Season to taste.

Cook the quail's eggs for 3 minutes in boiling water, cool under running water, peel and keep in salted water in the refrigerator.

Wash the samphire and the lettuce leaves. Arrange the salad leaves around the plate, place the samphire in a 12 cm/5 in circular pastry cutter in the centre of the plate. Layer the salmon on top of the samphire, halve the quail's eggs and use to decorate the salmon and samphire layer together with the borage flowers. Squeeze some lime juice onto the salmon and serve with a spoonful of dressing and a sprig of chervil.

Fat: high Kcals: 240 Cholesterol: high Fibre: low

Aubergine Gâteau with Provençale Vegetables

1 aubergine (eggplant)
juice of 1 lemon
2 dsp garlic oil

Provençale mix

1 courgette (zucchini)
1 red pepper
1 green pepper
1 yellow pepper
1 medium-sized onion
4 cloves garlic, roughly chopped

Sauce

2 beef tomatoes
2 dsp extra virgin olive oil
1 small onion, roughly chopped
50 ml/2 fl oz/¼ cup white wine
300 ml/10 fl oz/1¼ cups vegetable
    stock (see page 139)
1 sprig basil, shredded
1 sprig thyme

Garnish

25 g/1 oz/1¼ cup roasted pine
    kernels

Serves 4-6

Cut the aubergine (eggplant) into 6 mm/¼ in slices and cover with the lemon juice to prevent discoloration.

To make the sauce, quarter the tomatoes and sauté with half the olive oil. Add the onion and cook over a high heat for 1-2 minutes. Pour in the white wine and vegetable stock and simmer until the tomato is cooked thoroughly, approximately 10 minutes. After 5 minutes add the herbs. Purée the sauce in a food processor or liquidizer, then press through a fine sieve.

Cut all the vegetables for the Provençale mix into 1 cm/½ in dice. Heat the remaining oil in a frying pan (skillet), then add the diced vegetables and garlic and sauté until just beginning to soften. Bind with a little of the tomato sauce and remove from the heat.

In a separate pan sauté the aubergine (eggplant) slices in the garlic oil. Lightly brown each side and then drain on kitchen paper. Layer the Provençale mix with the aubergine (eggplant) slices, refrigerate, cover and press with a heavy weight or dish filled with cold water for 1 hour. Cut into wedges and serve garnished with pine kernels.

Fat: high Kcals: 224 Cholesterol: low Fibre: medium

Overleaf, from top: Endive Salad with Balsamic Honey Dressing, Smoked Salmon, Quails' Eggs and Samphire, Tomato and Olive Salad with Mango Dressing, and Wild Mushroom and Lentil Salad

Wild Mushroom and Lentil Salad

1 tsp walnut oil

3 rashers lean smoked back bacon,
    cut into lardons

350 g/12 oz small girolles, wiped

selection of salad leaves (e.g.
    rocket, endive, lollo rosso,
    oakleaf lettuce)

115 g/4 oz/¾ cup sprouting lentils

55 g/2 oz/¾ cup alfalfa sprouts

Dressing

1 bunch tarragon, blanched

150 ml/5 fl oz/⅔ cup natural, low-
    fat yoghurt (see page 142)

1 tsp clear honey

sea salt and cayenne pepper

Serves 4

Gently heat the walnut oil in a frying pan (skillet) and sauté the bacon lardons until crispy. Drain on kitchen paper. Add the girolles to the pan, sauté until soft and drain in the same way.

Chop the blanched tarragon, mix the yoghurt and honey together and season with salt and cayenne pepper. Wash the salad leaves and dress with half the yoghurt dressing. Mix the sprouting lentils with the mushrooms and bacon. Add the alfalfa sprouts to the remaining yoghurt, mix well and place in the centre of the plate.

To serve, arrange the salad leaves on top of the alfafa and yoghurt mixture and sprinkle the mushrooms, bacon lardons and lentils around the edge.

Fat: high Kcals: 159 Cholesterol: low Fibre: low

Tomato and Olive Salad with Mango Dressing

4 plum tomatoes

4 yellow cherry tomatoes

4 red cherry tomatoes

32 black olives

1 bunch chives, cut into batons

Dressing

1 mango

2 dsp white wine vinegar

2 dsp extra virgin olive oil

4 basil leaves, shredded

sea salt and freshly milled black
    pepper

Garnish

4 sprigs each of purple and green
    basil

Serves 4

Blanch all the tomatoes together for 10 seconds, refresh under cold running water and remove the skins.

To make the dressing, peel the mango and place the flesh into a liquidizer or food processor with the vinegar. Blend until smooth, then slowly add the olive oil while the machine is running. Pass through a fine chinois and add the shredded basil. Season with a small amount of salt and black pepper, and add a little water if the dressing is too thick.

To assemble the salad, arrange the different tomatoes attractively on a plate with the olives in the centre, season with a little salt and pepper. Sprinkle the chive batons onto the salad and finish with a circle of dressing surrounding the salad. Garnish with purple and green basil.

Fat: medium Kcals: 108 Cholesterol: low Fibre: low

Onion, Fennel, Apple and Horseradish Salad

1 tsp sesame oil

2 bulbs fennel, cut into thin slices across the bulb

1 red apple, cut into 6 mm/¼ in dice

1 green apple, cut into 6 mm/¼ in dice

2 small red onions

2 tbsp sultanas

1 orange, segmented

½ head radicchio

sea salt and freshly milled black pepper

Dressing

1 tbsp clear honey

1 tsp fresh horseradish, grated

150 ml/5 fl oz/⅔ cup natural, low-fat yoghurt (see page 142)

juice of ½ lemon

Garnish

1 tbsp poppy seeds

Serves 4

Heat the sesame oil in a wok or deep frying pan (skillet) until smoking. Add the fennel and stir-fry for 1 minute. Drain on kitchen paper and leave to cool.

To make the dressing, mix the honey, horseradish and yoghurt together, add the lemon juice and season with salt and pepper.

Toss all the other ingredients together in a large bowl. Divide the radicchio between the plates, place a quarter of the salad on top, dress and garnish with poppy seeds.

Fat: low Kcals: 156 Cholesterol: low Fibre: medium

Glazed Onion and Wild Mushroom Tartlets

170 g/6 oz wholemeal pastry (see page 144)

1 tbsp extra virgin olive oil

2 Spanish onions, finely sliced

225 g/8 oz/3 cups mixed wild mushrooms, wiped

1 clove garlic, finely diced (minced)

2 tbsp balsamic vinegar

1 tbsp maple syrup

675 g/1½ lb button onions, peeled

150 ml/5 fl oz/⅔ cup vegetable stock (see page 139)

sea salt and freshly milled black pepper

Preheat the oven to 150°C/300°F/gas 2. Place a baking sheet in the oven to heat.

Grease 4 × 10 cm/4 in fluted pastry rings. On a lightly floured surface roll out the pastry and cut circles to fit the rings. Bake blind for 10 minutes and set the tartlets to one side to cool.

Heat half the oil in a pan and sweat the onions until golden brown. Spoon a quarter of the onions into each pastry case. In a non-stick pan sweat the wild mushrooms, garlic, balsamic vinegar, maple syrup and the remaining olive oil over a medium heat until cooked, approximately 5 minutes.

In a separate pan cook the button onions in the vegetable stock over a medium heat for 5 minutes. Strain both the cooking liquids for the mushrooms and the onions into another pan.

Arrange a quarter of the onions in a circle on the base of each tartlet

Garnish
1 bunch chervil

Serves 4

and pile the wild mushrooms in the centre. Season the sauce with salt and black pepper and reduce over a high heat to a sticky glaze. If necessary, add a little more maple syrup to thicken it. Pour the sauce over each tartlet, then bake in the oven for 10 minutes to warm through. Serve garnished with chervil.

Fat: high Kcals: 312 Cholesterol: low Fibre: high

Pasta, Cured Ham, Rocket, Garlic and Basil Salad

350 g/12 oz wholemeal pasta (see
     page 140)
1 tsp lemon juice
1 bunch rocket
30 g/1 oz Parma ham
1 medium-sized onion, finely
     chopped
1 clove garlic, finely diced (minced)
2 tsp fresh parsley, chopped
sea salt and freshly milled black
     pepper

Dressing
½ bunch basil
4 dsp extra virgin olive oil
1 tbsp cider vinegar
1 tsp Dijon mustard
juice of 1 lemon

Garnish
1 dsp Parmesan cheese, grated
4 sprigs basil

Serves 4

Roll out the pasta as thinly as possible by machine or hand. Cut into tagliatelle. Bring a large pan of water to the boil with a teaspoon of the lemon juice and drop in the pasta. Cook for 3 minutes, then drain.

Meanwhile, make the dressing. Combine three-quarters of the basil, the olive oil, cider vinegar, mustard, salt to taste and the lemon juice in a liquidizer or food processor and process until smooth, then pass through a fine sieve.

Reserve 8 whole rocket leaves and cut the rest into 5 cm/2 in pieces and place in a large bowl. Cut the Parma ham into fine strips and add to the bowl. Then add the drained pasta and all the other ingredients. Toss with the dressing. To serve, on each plate place 2 whole rocket leaves, put a quarter of the salad on top, sprinkle over a teaspoon of Parmesan and finish with a sprig of basil.

Fat: high Kcals: 322 Cholesterol: low Fibre: medium

Above: *Marinated Grilled Vegetables;* opposite, top: *Glazed Onion and Wild Mushroom Tartlet;* opposite, bottom: *Feta Cheese, Leek, Potato and Yoghurt Tartlet*

Feta Cheese, Leek, Potato and Yoghurt Tartlets

4 sheets ready-made filo pastry

1 egg white

1 small leek, finely diced (minced)

1 clove garlic, finely diced (minced)

4 small new potatoes

55 g/2 oz/1 cup feta cheese

150 ml/5 oz/⅔ cup natural, low-fat
 yoghurt (see page 142)

2 eggs

1 tsp walnut oil

1 bunch chives, finely chopped

a selection of salad leaves

sea salt and freshly milled black
 pepper

Garnish

2 pickled walnuts, cut in halves

1 bunch flowering marjoram

Serves 4

Preheat the oven to 190°C/375°F/gas 5.

Brush 2 sheets of filo pastry with a little egg white and line 4 7.5 cm/3 in tartlet moulds with 2 layers of pastry.

Sweat the leek in a non-stick pan with the garlic until it is softened. Mix the potatoes, lightly scrubbed and grated, leeks and garlic and feta cheese together and place in the pastry cases.

Mix the yoghurt with the egg, add the chives and season to taste. Pour into the pastry cases and bake for 15 minutes.

Gently ease the cases from the moulds and serve with the torn salad leaves tossed in the walnut oil. Serve garnished with marjoram flowers and the pickled walnut halves.

Fat: medium Kcals: 188 Cholesterol: high Fibre: low

Marinated Grilled Vegetables

1 large carrot

4 shallots

4 asparagus tips

1 red pepper

1 yellow pepper

1 green pepper

2 small courgettes (zucchini)

2 sticks celery

1 medium-sized leek

½ small aubergine (eggplant)

8 baby corn

1 bulb fennel

225 g/8 oz/1 cup wild rice

6 tbsp tomato vinaigrette (see
    page 136)

sea salt and freshly milled black
    pepper

Marinade

150 ml/5 fl oz/⅔ cup extra virgin
    olive oil

1 bunch basil, shredded

3 cloves garlic

150 ml/5 fl oz/⅔ cup dry white wine

juice of 1 lemon

Serves 4

Mix together all the marinade ingredients. Peel and chop all the vegetables into bite-sized pieces and place in a shallow dish. Spoon over the marinade and leave to marinate in a cool place for 4 hours, turning occasionally.

Thirty minutes before the end of the marinating time, rinse the wild rice in cold water. Bring a large pan of water to the boil and add the rice. Cover and simmer for 40 minutes until cooked. Drain and fluff up the grains with a fork. Keep warm.

Strain the marinade off the vegetables and place under a hot grill or on a barbecue for approximately 5 minutes until crisp and brown.

Divide the rice evenly between the plates, place the vegetables on top and pour round some tomato vinaigrette.

Fat: high Kcals: 448 Cholesterol: low Fibre: high

Vegetable and Nut Croquettes

2 tbsp hazelnut oil

1 clove garlic, finely diced (minced)

2 small courgettes (zucchini), grated

1 small carrot, grated

1 small onion, grated

1 dsp walnuts, chopped

1 dsp hazelnuts, chopped

1 bunch parsley

1 dsp smooth peanut butter

1 dsp poppy seeds

1 dsp sesame seeds

Sauce

1 red pepper

1 green pepper

2 small potatoes

1 sprig thyme

2 bay leaves

300 ml/10 fl oz/1¼ cups vegetable
    stock (see page 139)

1 dash chilli sauce

juice of ½ lemon

sea salt and freshly milled black
    pepper

Garnish

4 sprigs chervil

Serves 4

Preheat the oven to 180°C/350°F/gas 4.

Heat 1 tablespoon of the hazelnut oil in a pan and sweat the garlic and grated vegetables over a low heat until lightly cooked but still crisp. Add the chopped nuts, parsley and peanut butter and cook for 2 minutes over a low heat. Place the mixture on a clean tea towel and squeeze all the moisture from the vegetables. Roll the dry mixture into 8 croquette sausage shapes. Mix together the poppy and sesame seeds and roll the croquettes in the mixture.

To make the sauce, place the red and green peppers in separate pans with 1 potato in each. Divide all the other ingredients equally between the 2 pans and add a dash of chilli sauce to the red pepper mixture only. Bring both pans to the boil, cover and simmer for 15 minutes until the potato is cooked. Purée the 2 sauces separately in a food processor or blender and pass each through a fine sieve into individual pans. Season with lemon juice, salt and pepper.

Heat the remaining hazelnut oil in a small frying pan (skillet) and brown the croquettes. Place them on a baking sheet and cook in the oven for 12 minutes until golden brown. To serve, spoon a pool of each sauce onto a plate, place 2 croquettes on top and garnish with a sprig of chervil.

Fat: high Kcals: 214 Cholesterol: low Fibre: medium

Above: *Asparagus and Broccoli Charlotte; opposite Celeriac Spring Rolls*

Asparagus and Broccoli Charlotte

30 thin green asparagus spears
30 thin white asparagus spears
250 g/8½ oz broccoli heads
4 eggs
300 ml/10 fl oz/1¼ cups natural,
  low-fat *fromage frais*
sea salt and freshly milled white
  pepper

Sauce

1 potato, peeled and roughly
  chopped
575 ml/20 fl oz/2½ cups fresh
  orange juice
1 cardamom pod (bean), crushed
½ clove garlic, finely diced (minced)
½ bay leaf

To make the sauce, place all the ingredients except the tarragon and the *fromage frais* in a pan and reduce over a high heat by two-thirds, about 20 minutes. Stir in the *fromage frais* and pass through a fine sieve. Season to taste.

To make the charlottes, lightly grease 4 ramekins and line with greaseproof (wax) paper. Cut away the woody ends from the asparagus, then trim the tips into 4 cm/1½ in lengths; reserve the stalks for the mousse. Using string, tie the tips into bundles and blanch in plenty of salted water for 1 minute, then refresh under cold running water and drain. Discard the strings. Cut half the broccoli heads into florets and blanch as before.

To make the mousse, cook the other half of the broccoli heads with the asparagus stalks until tender. Refresh under cold running water, drain, then combine with the eggs and *fromage frais* in a liquidizer or food processor and blend until smooth. Season to taste.

Preheat the oven to 180°C/350°F/gas 4. Line the ramekins with asparagus tips, alternating green and white spears. Spoon the mousse

1 tsp fresh tarragon, chopped
2 tsp natural, low-fat *fromage frais*

Garnish
1 tomato sliced

Serves 4

mixture into the ramekins and smooth level. Place the broccoli florets around the top. Cook in a *bain marie* in the oven for 25 minutes until slightly risen. Leave to rest for 5 minutes. Meanwhile, reheat the sauce and stir in the chopped tarragon. Plunge each ramekin into hot water for 30 seconds up to the rim and turn out the charlottes onto a plate. Surround with a little of the sauce and slices of tomato. Serve immediately.

Fat: medium Kcals: 300 Cholesterol: high Fibre: high

Celeriac Spring Rolls

1 × 2.5 cm/1 in square fresh ginger, peeled

1 bunch spring onions (scallions)

2 dsp sesame oil

1 large head celeriac, cut into paper-thin strips, blanched in salted water

55 g/2 oz/½ cup bean sprouts

2 medium-sized carrots, cut into thin strips

1 small onion, sliced

1 red pepper, cut into strips

8 water chestnuts, sliced

1 clove garlic, finely diced (minced)

2 tsp light soy sauce

1 egg white

Sauce

450 g/1 lb overripe plums

1 bay leaf

1 clove garlic, finely diced (minced)

1 star anise

1 stick cinnamon

1 tsp fresh ginger, peeled and chopped

25 g/1 oz/⅓ cup fresh raspberries

1 tbsp lemon juice

1 dsp raw cane sugar

2 dsp sake or dry sherry

Makes 12 rolls

Place all the sauce ingredients in a thick-bottomed pan and cook over a high heat for 20 minutes. Cool and pass through a muslin cloth.

Cut the ginger into fine strips, blanch, then refresh 6 times under cold running water. Cut the spring onions (scallions) into 5 cm/2 in pieces, blanch separately and refresh once. Heat the sesame oil in a frying pan (skillet) and stir-fry all the vegetables until lightly cooked but still crisp. Season with soy sauce and leave to cool. Drain the celeriac slices on kitchen paper.

Place a little filling in the centre of each celeriac slice, brush the edges with a little egg white and roll up like a pancake, tucking in and securing the ends neatly.

To serve, arrange 3 rolls on each plate, spoon over the sauce, and scatter around the spring onions and ginger strips.

Fat: low Kcals: 60 Cholesterol: low Fibre: low

Celeriac and Wild Mushroom Terrine

1.5 kg/3½ lb courgettes (zucchini), grated

1.35 kg/3 lb celeriac, grated

2 tsp extra virgin olive oil

1 kg/2¼ lb onions, roughly chopped

1 clove garlic, finely diced (minced)

450 g/16 oz mixed wild mushrooms, wiped

1 dash Worcester sauce

Garnish

150 ml/5 fl oz/⅔ cup apple purée, made by boiling 3 eating apples with 2 tbsps water until soft, and then passed through a fine sieve

1 red pepper, finely chopped

Serves 14

Line a 1.1 litre/2 pint/5 cup terrine with cling film or plastic wrap. Sweat the grated courgette (zucchini) and celeriac in a large pan with a little salt and pepper until soft.

Heat half the olive oil in a separate pan, add the onions, garlic, wild mushrooms (reserve 8 for garnishing) and a dash of Worcester sauce and sweat until the onions become translucent.

To assemble the terrine, line the base with a thin layer of courgette (zucchini) and celeriac, then a layer of the mushroom mixture, followed by another layer of courgette (zucchini) and celeriac and so on until all the ingredients are used up.

Wrap cling film or plastic wrap over the top of the terrine, then pierce a few small holes thorough the film to allow liquid to escape while the terrine is being pressed. Place a heavy weight or dish filled with cold water on top of the terrine and leave in the refrigerator for at least 2 hours.

To remove the terrine from the mould, invert on to a serving plate. Place a generous slice in the centre of each plate, accompanied by the apple purée, the remaining olive oil, reserved mushrooms and chopped red pepper.

Fat: low Kcals: 92 Cholesterol: low Fibre: medium

Desserts

Desserts provide the perfect end to any meal. This section includes a mixture of simple sweets, old favourites, elegant desserts and special treats, such as Kiwi and Orange Slice with Sweet Vinaigrette, Poached Peaches with Cinnamon Ice Cream, and Banana and Sultana Mousse, that will leave guests feeling refreshed and satisfied.

Frozen Wild Strawberry and Yoghurt Terrine

350 g/12 oz/3 cups wild
   strawberries
4 sheets gelatine
300 ml/10 fl oz/1¼ cup ice cream
   (see page 143)
300 ml/10 fl oz/1¼ cup natural, low-
   fat yoghurt (see page 142)
3 egg whites

Garnish
zest of 1 lemon, cut into thin strips
1 tbsp clear honey

Serves 14

Place a third of the strawberries in a heavy-bottomed saucepan with a little water and boil until puréed.

Meanwhile, cover the sheet gelatine with cold water and leave to soften for approximately 5 minutes. Remove from the water with your hand and squeeze out any excess liquid, then place the gelatine in small heatproof bowl over a pan of barely simmering water. Leave until the gelatine has melted and turned transparent. Stir into the puréed strawberries, and strain through a muslin cloth into a 1.1 litre/2 pint/5 cup terrine. Chill in the refrigerator until set, 30 minutes.

Reserve 12 strawberries for the garnish, and liquidize the rest in a liquidizer or food processor and blend with the ice cream which has been transferred to the refrigerator half an hour beforehand to soften slightly. Stir in the yoghurt and leave to cool.

In a clean, dry bowl, whisk the egg whites until stiff and fold into the ice cream mixture, using a large metal spoon. Spoon into the terrine and transfer to the freezer for 3 hours.

To serve, slightly warm the terrine and turn it out onto a clean board. Cut into 2 cm/¾ in slices and place a slice on each plate. Heat the honey with 1 tablespoon of water and blanch the strips of lemon zest in this mixture for 4 minutes. Refresh in cold water and use as a garnish together with the reserved strawberries. Serve immediately.

Fat: low Kcals: 48 Cholesterol: low Fibre: low

Opposite, from back: *Banana and Sultana Mousse, Rhubarb Charlotte, and Frozen Wild Strawberry and Yoghurt Terrine*

Banana and Sultana Mousse

1 quantity honey tuile (see page 144)

30 g/1 oz/¼ cup carob chips

5 sheets gelatine

300 ml/10 fl oz/1¼ cups *crème anglaise* (see page 142)

2 large ripe bananas

45 g/1½ oz/¼ cup sultanas

40 ml/1½ fl oz/¼ cup dark rum

3 tbsp natural, low-fat *fromage frais*

zest of ½ lemon, finely diced and blanched in 1 tbsp honey and 1 tbsp water

1 tsp raw cane sugar

Garnish

115 g/4 oz/1 cup raspberries

½ bunch mint (optional)

Serves 4

Preheat the oven to 180°C/350°F/gas 4.

Spread the tuile on a baking sheet to form 2 rectangles, each measuring at least 13 cm × 50 cm/5 in × 20 in, and sprinkle over the carob chips. Cook in the oven for 4 minutes until golden. Remove from the oven and immediately cut the tuile into 4 rectangles 6.5 cm x 25 cm/2½ in × 10 in and wrap each rectangle around the outside of a small ramekin. Remove the honey tuile shapes from the ramekin as soon as they have cooled and hardened.

Cover the sheet gelatine with cold water and leave to soften for approximately 5 minutes. Remove from the water with your hand and squeeze out any excess liquid, then place the gelatine in a small heatproof bowl. Put the bowl into a pan of barely simmering water and leave until the gelatine has melted and turned transparent. Warm the *crème anglaise*, add the gelatine and stir thoroughly. Put half the *crème anglaise* to one side, and combine the other half with 2 of the bananas in a food processor or liquidizer and process until smooth, then press through a fine sieve. Leave to cool.

Place the sultanas with three-quarters of the rum in a pan, bring to the boil and cook for 4 minutes until the sultanas are plump and the rum absorbed. Reserve a few sultanas for garnishing and add the rest to the *crème anglaise* and banana purée, stirring in well. Stir in the *fromage frais* and the lemon zest and spoon into the 4 ramekins. Place in the refrigerator.

Thinly slice the remaining banana and sprinkle with the sugar. Place under a preheated hot grill and cook until golden brown. Leave to one side to cool.

Meanwhile, set aside 4 sprigs of mint for garnishing and finely shred the rest. Add to the reserved *crème anglaise*, stir in the rest of the rum and when cool press through a fine sieve.

Plunge the base of each ramekin into hot water for 30 seconds and turn the mousses out onto individual plates and wrap a honey tuile shape around the outside. Arrange slices of the grilled banana on top, then garnish with a few sultanas, and a sprig of mint if liked. Liquidize the raspberries in a food processor or blender, press through a fine sieve and pour round. Add a sprig of mint, if liked.

Fat: high Kcals: 472 Cholesterol: medium Fibre: low

Rhubarb Charlotte

1 dsp strawberry preserve

8 sheets gelatine

150 ml/5 fl oz/⅔ cup warm *crème anglaise*

4 dsp natural, low-fat *fromage frais*

450 g/1 lb rhubarb, chopped

1 tsp low-calorie granulated sweetener

150 ml/5 fl oz/⅔ cup red grape juice

Sponge

55 g/2 oz/¼ cup caster sugar

2 eggs

55 g/2 oz/½ cup wholemeal flour

30 g/1 oz/⅛ cup polyunsaturated margarine, melted

Serves 4

Preheat the oven to 205°C/400°F/gas 6. Line a shallow roasting tray with greaseproof (wax) paper.

To make the sponge mixture, whisk the sugar and eggs together until thick and creamy. Using a large metal spoon, fold in the flour and then the melted margarine. Spread the mixture into the lined tray, making sure it is in an even layer, approximately 6 mm/¼ in thick. Bake in the oven until golden brown and spongy to the touch. Turn out on to a wire rack and leave to cool. Peel off the greaseproof (wax) paper and cut the sponge into strips 2.5 cm/1 in thick. Spread the strawberry preserve onto the strips and sandwich together. Cut the strips widthways to leave lengths of approximately 6mm/¼ in.

Cover the gelatine with cold water for approximately 5 minutes to soften. Remove the gelatine from the water and squeeze out any excess liquid with your hand. Melt the gelatine in a *bain marie* and stir into the *crème anglaise*. Add two-thirds of the gelatine to the *fromage frais* and keep the rest liquid in the *bain marie*. Stew the chopped rhubarb in a covered pan over a low heat until soft. Add the sweetener and mix in a food processor or blender until smooth. Pass through a fine sieve, stir into the *crème anglaise* mixture and leave to cool.

In a separate pan warm the grape juice and add the remaining gelatine to it. Line 4 ramekins with this mixture to a depth of 6 mm/¼ in. Leave to set in the refrigerator, about 30 minutes. When set, line the inside of each ramekin with the sponge, placing the strips vertically. Fill the ramekins with the rhubarb mixture and leave to set in the refrigerator for at least 2 hours.

To serve, briefly plunge the base of each ramekin up to its rim in hot water. Place a plate upside down over the ramekin, smartly invert, giving a couple of sharp shakes if necessary to free the charlottes.

Fat: high Kcals: 269 Cholesterol: high Fibre: low

Apricot and Passion Fruit Water Ice

170 g/6 oz/¾ cup dried apricots
6 passion fruit
300 ml/10 fl oz/1¼ cup fresh orange
    juice
juice of 1 lemon

Garnish
4 sprigs fresh mint

Serves 4

Place the apricots in a pan, cover with water and bring to the boil. Simmer, covered, for 20 minutes or until the fruit is soft.

Scoop out the seeds from the passion fruit into a separate pan, add the orange juice and reduce by two-thirds over a high heat.

Drain the apricots and purée in a food processor or liquidizer. Stir in the passion fruit and orange mixture and blend again until well mixed. Press through a fine sieve into an ice cream maker or *sorbetière* and add sufficient lemon juice to reach the consistency of olive oil. Churn for 10 minutes, or until stiff. Store in a covered container in the freezer. If you do not have an ice cream maker, after adding the lemon juice, place the mixture in a container directly into the freezer. Whisk every 15-20 minutes for 3-4 hours until set. The water ice can be stored for up to 3 days in the freezer in a sealed container.

Serve in scoops garnished with sprigs of mint.

Fat: low Kcals: 105 Cholesterol: low Fibre: low

Raspberry and Strawberry Layer

1 quantity honey tuile (see page
    144)
115 g/4 oz/1 cup strawberries,
    liquidized and strained
150 ml/5 fl oz/⅔ cup natural, low-
    fat *fromage frais*
1 vanilla pod
2 sheets gelatine
225 g/8 oz/2 cups raspberries

Garnish
icing (confectioner's) sugar, for
    dusting
85 g/3 oz/¾ cup strawberries,
    sliced
4 sprigs fresh mint

Serves 4

Make 15 circular honey tuile biscuits and leave to cool.

Mix the strawberry pulp with the *fromage frais* and the seeds from the vanilla pod.

Cover the gelatine with cold water and leave to soften for approximately 5 minutes. Remove from the water with your hand and squeeze out any excess liquid, then place the gelatine in a heatproof bowl. Put the bowl, in a pan of barely simmering water until the gelatine has melted and turned transparent.

Gently warm the *fromage frais* and strawberry mixture and stir in the gelatine. (You may need slightly more gelatine to set the mixture if the *fromage frais* is thin.) Place in the refrigerator to set.

Once set, place the mixture in a piping bag fitted with a medium nozzle, arrange the raspberries around a biscuit on each plate and pipe a little of the mousse in the centre of the tuile. Sandwich the biscuits together with layers of strawberry mousse and top with a plain biscuit. Dust the top of the final biscuit with icing (confectioner's) sugar, surround with sliced strawberries and decorate with a spring of mint.

Fat: high Kcals: 191 Cholesterol: low Fibre: high

Opposite: *Délice of Raspberries and Nectarine*

Bread and Fruit Pudding with Banana Sauce

12 thin slices wholemeal bread
1 tsp polyunsaturated spread
25 g/1 oz/⅓ cup fresh blueberries
1 tsp mixed spice
1 ripe banana, finely chopped
1 egg
1 tbsp clear honey
300 ml/½ pt/1¼ cups skimmed milk
½ vanilla pod

Sauce
500 ml/16 fl oz/2 cups fresh orange
    juice
2 small, overripe bananas, roughly
    chopped
½ vanilla pod, deseeded

Garnish
4 sprigs fresh mint

Serves 4

Grease 4 individual ramekins. Cut 12 circular-shaped slices of bread, using the ramekins as a template. Spread both sides of the circles of bread with the spread. Lay one circle in each ramekin.

Divide the blueberries into 4, lay on top of the bread and sprinkle with a pinch of mixed spice. Place another circle of bread on top of the fruit and press down firmly.

Divide the chopped banana into 4 and place on top of the next layer of bread. Place the third circle of bread on top and push down firmly.

Whisk the egg, honey and milk together and add the vanilla pod seeds, scraping them from the pod with the back of a knife. Carefully pour the egg custard over the puddings, waiting for the custard to soak through the layers until it reaches the rim of the ramekin. Place in the refrigerator until ready to bake.

Preheat the oven to 180°C/350°F/gas 4.

To make the sauce, put the orange juice, roughly chopped banana and vanilla pod in a pan and reduce over a high heat by two-thirds. Take off the heat, remove the vanilla pod and process in a food processor or blender until smooth. Pass through a fine sieve and keep warm.

Bake the puddings in the oven for 12 minutes until golden. Turn out into 4 individual bowls and pour over the warm sauce. Garnish with a sprig of fresh mint and serve.

Fat: low Kcals: 339 Cholesterol: medium Fibre: medium

Apricot, Fig and Coconut Terrine

4 dried figs
12 dried apricots
50 g/2 oz carob
1 passion fruit
1 tbsp clear honey
2 tbsp desiccated (shredded)
    coconut, toasted
icing (confectioner's) sugar,
    for dusting

Garnish
berry fruits

Serves 6

Roughly chop the figs, 4 of the apricots, and half the carob in a food processor or blender. Stir in the passion fruit seeds and the honey. Press into a 575 ml/1 pint/2½ cup terrine and freeze for 30 minutes.

To make the apricot purée, dice (mince) the remaining 8 dried apricots, place in a pan and just cover with water. Bring to the boil, cover and simmer for 20-30 minutes. Purée in a food processor or blender.

Melt the remaining carob in a *bain marie* and spread in a thin layer on greaseproof (wax) paper and place in the refrigerator. When set, trim with a hot knife into a 5 cm × 3 cm/2 in × 1¼ in rectangle. Remove from the paper and dip one side in the toasted coconut.

Run a sharp knife around the edge of the terrine and turn out the fruit onto a plate. Pour the apricot purée around the terrine and decorate with berry fruits as required. Dust the berry fruits with icing (confectioner's) sugar. Place the carob rectangle on top and serve.

Fat: low Kcals: 43 Cholesterol: low Fibre: low

Champneys Apple Crumble with Honey-Sweetened Fromage Frais

450 g/1 lb cooking apples, peeled,
    cored and roughly chopped
1 tsp ground cinnamon
45 g/1½ oz/¼ cup polyunsaturated
    spread
a little fresh orange juice, to mix
85 g/3 oz/¾ cup wholemeal flour
20 g/¾ oz/1½ tbsp rolled oats
20 g/¾ oz/½ tbsp raw cane caster
    sugar
6 tbsp natural, low-fat *fromage frais*
½ tbsp clear honey

Serves 4

Preheat the oven to 150°C/300°F/gas 2.

Place the apple, cinnamon and half of the polyunsaturated spread in a pan and cover. Gently sweat, mashing the fruit from time to time, until puréed. Add a little orange juice if the fruit begins to stick to the pan. Once cooked, keep the purée hot over a gentle heat.

Meanwhile, in a mixing bowl, rub together the flour, oats, sugar and the rest of the polyunsaturated spread until the mixture resembles breadcrumbs. Divide the mixture into 4 and lightly press into a 5 cm/2 in circular pastry cutter to form 4 circles. Lift away the cutter and place the circles on a greased baking sheet and bake in the oven for 20 minutes, until golden brown. Transfer to a wire rack.

While the pastry is cooking, whisk together the *fromage frais* and honey. Chill.

To serve, place a clean 5 cm/2 in pastry cutter onto the first plate and spoon in hot apple purée to the rim. Press down gently, then remove the cutter and place a crumble circle on top. Serve the sweetened *fromage frais* separately.

Fat: high Kcals: 248 Cholesterol: low Fibre: low

Pumpkin and Pear Pie

900 g/2 lb pumpkin
1 pinch nutmeg
1 tbsp low-calorie, granulated
    sweetener
225 g/8 oz wholemeal pastry (see
    page 144)
3 egg whites
6 tbsp low-fat, natural *fromage frais*
4 ripe pears
100 ml/4 fl oz/½ cup red wine
2 cinnamon sticks

Serves 6

Preheat the oven to 180°C/350°F/gas 4.

Peel and roughly chop the pumpkin and place in a pan with 2 tablespoons of water and the nutmeg. Cook until soft, about 20 minutes, stir in the sweetener and leave to cool.

Roll out the pastry on a clean, flat surface and line a 25 cm/10 in pie tin. Bake blind for 10 minutes until the pastry is pale gold.

Add the egg whites and *fromage frais* to the pumpkin mixture and mix in a food processor or blender until smooth, then pass through a sieve.

Peel the pears and place in a deep pan with the wine, 1 tablespoon of water and the cinnamon sticks. Poach lightly for approximately 25 minutes. Remove from the poaching liquid and set aside to cool. When cool, halve the pears and remove the core.

Place the pumpkin mixture in the pastry case, put the pears on top and bake for 30-35 minutes until golden brown.

Fat: high Kcals: 220 Cholesterol: low Fibre: high

Délice of Raspberries and Nectarine

2 eggs

55 g/2 oz/¼ cup raw cane sugar

55 g/2 oz/½ cup wholemeal flour

1 tsp cocoa powder

4 ripe nectarines

1 tsp clear honey

1 star anise

115 g/4 oz/1 cup raspberries

juice of ½ lemon

300 ml/10 fl oz/1¼ cups natural,
    low-fat *fromage frais*

1 vanilla pod

6 sheets gelatine

55 g/2 oz carob

Garnish

4 sprigs mint

Serves 4

Preheat the oven to 180°C/350°F/gas 4. Place a baking sheet in the oven to heat.

Whisk the eggs and sugar in a heatproof bowl placed over a pan of barely simmering water until the mixture is almost white. Remove from the heat and fold in the flour, using a large metal spoon. Halve the mixture and stir in the cocoa powder into one half. Line 2 x 450 ml/16 fl oz/2 cup terrines with the sponge mixture, one chocolate and one plain. Bake in the oven for 12 minutes until pale gold.

Reserve 1 nectarine for garnishing, and roughly chop up the rest, discarding the stones. Place the chopped nectarines in a pan with the honey and star anise and simmer for 15 minutes until the nectarines are soft. Pass through a muslin cloth and reserve 3 teaspoons of the purée for garnishing.

Reserve 12 raspberries for garnishing; in a separate pan, cook the rest with the lemon juice until a purée is formed, then pass through a muslin cloth. Reserve 4 teaspoons for garnishing.

Place the *fromage frais* and the seeds from the vanilla pod in a metal bowl, place over a pan of boiling water and heat to blood temperature, 37°C/96°F.

Cover the sheet gelatine with cold water and leave to soften for approximately 5 minutes. Remove from the water with your hand and squeeze out any excess liquid, then place the gelatine in a small heatproof bowl. Put the bowl into a pan of barely simmering water and leave until the gelatine has melted and turned transparent. Stir into the *fromage frais*, then halve and stir the raspberry purée into one half and the nectarine purée into the other.

Pour the raspberry mixture into the chocolate–lined terrine, and the nectarine mixture into the plain one. Place in the refrigerator to set.

Melt the carob in a *bain marie* and place in a piping bag. Pipe 2 circles onto a large dessert plate. Remove the terrines from the refrigerator, turn out onto a board and cut each one into 1 cm/½ in slices On each plate, fill 1 circle of carob with a quarter of the reserved nectarine purée and the other circle with a quarter of the reserved raspberry purée. Place a slice of raspberry terrine on the circle of nectarine purée, and a slice of nectarine terrine on the circle of raspberry purée. Cut the reserved nectarine into 12 slices. Garnish the plate with 3 nectarine slices and 3 raspberries, and top with a sprig of mint.

Fat: low Kcals: 277 Cholesterol: high Fibre: medium

Kiwi and Orange Slice with Sweet Vinaigrette

2 tbsp caster sugar
2 tbsp polyunsaturated spread
2 egg whites
25 g/1 oz/⅓ cup wholemeal flour
2 kiwi fruit, peeled and finely sliced
2 oranges, peeled and segmented
50 ml/2 fl oz/¼ cup *crème fraîche*,
    sweetened with a little honey

Vinaigrette

2 tbsp maple syrup
1 tsp white wine vinegar
2 tbsp white wine
1 strawberry, diced (minced)
4 mint leaves, finely shredded

Garnish

zest of 1 orange, blanched

Serves 6

Beat the caster sugar and polyunsaturated spread together until white and creamy. Beat in the egg whites, then stir in the flour in batches. Place the mixture in the refrigerator for 1 hour.

Preheat the oven to 175°C/325°F/gas 3 or 180°C/350°F/gas 4.

Grease a baking sheet. Using a tablespoon, drop 12 mounds of mixture onto the baking sheet, spacing them 2.5 cm/1 in apart. Spread each mound out thinly, using a flat knife, to form circles approximately 10 cm/4 in in diameter. Bake in the oven for 4 minutes, until pale gold. Transfer the biscuits to a wire rack to cool.

To make the vinaigrette, mix all the ingredients together in a serving bowl until well blended.

To assemble each serving, start with a biscuit at the base. Place a layer of kiwi and orange on top, then repeat with two more layers of biscuit and fruit, finishing with a layer of fruit. Pipe sweetened *crème fraîche* in the centre. Serve the sweet vinaigrette and blanched orange zest separately.

Fat: medium Kcals: 138 Cholesterol: low Fibre: low

Banana en Papillote

4 small, underripe bananas
1 cinnamon stick, cut into 4
4 star anise
1 vanilla pod, cut into 4
30 g/1 oz/2 tbsp carob, grated
75 ml/3 fl oz/½ cup pineapple juice

Serves 4

Preheat the oven to 230°C/450°F/gas 8.

Lightly grease a piece of aluminium foil large enough to cover 1 banana, and place a banana on top. Arrange a piece of cinnamon stick, 1 star anise and a piece of vanilla pod around the banana and sprinkle with grated carob and a quarter of the pineapple juice. Fold up the foil and seal to make an airtight pocket. Repeat the process with the other 3 bananas.

Place the sealed bananas on a baking tray and cook in the oven for 3-4 minutes. Alternatively, they can be cooked on the side of a bonfire. Serve immediately.

Fat: low Kcals: 92 Cholesterol: low Fibre: low

A Tulip of Passion Fruit and Apricot Sorbet with Fresh Fruits

100 g/3½ oz/½ cup dried apricots

150 ml/5 fl oz/⅔ cup fresh orange
   juice

3 passion fruit

juice of 1 lemon

Tulip basket

8 sheets ready-made filo pastry

1 tbsp clear honey

Selection of fruits

1 star fruit, sliced

4 strawberries, sliced

1 orange, segmented

1 red apple, sliced

Fruit sauce

6 strawberries

1 tsp clear honey

juice of ½ lemon

Garnish

flesh of 2 melons, scooped into
   small balls

zest of 1 orange, blanched and cut
   into strips

Serves 4

To make the sorbet, boil the apricots in the orange juice with the seeds of the passion fruit until soft, 20–30 minutes. Purée the softened fruit in a food processor or blender and then add the lemon juice. Adjust the consistency of the fruit purée with more orange juice so that it resembles thick cooking oil. Place in a large bowl and put in the freezer. Stir every hour until set, approximately 3–4 hours. Alternatively place in an ice cream maker or *sorbetière* until firm.

Preheat the oven to 180°C/350°F/gas 4. Put a baking sheet in the oven to heat.

To make the fruit sauce, place all the ingredients in a food processor or blender and mix until smooth. Pass through a sieve into a clean bowl and keep cool.

Cut the filo pastry into 8 circles, approximately 13 cm/5 in in radius. Gently heat the honey in a small pan and use half to brush 4 of the filo circles. Top each honeyed circle with another to form a double layer. Push each circle into a deep jam tart or muffin tin, making sure that the base is flat. Place on the baking sheet and bake for 5 minutes. Brush with the remaining honey, return to the oven and bake until golden brown, approximately 2 minutes. Remove from the tin and cool on a wire rack.

To serve, spoon a little of the sorbet into each tulip basket and add the sliced fruit and strawberry purée around the sorbet. Garnish with the melon balls and strips of blanched orange zest.

Fat: low Kcals: 198 Cholesterol: low Fibre: high

Pineapple and Almond Soufflé

300 ml/10 fl oz/1¼ cups skimmed
   milk

1 vanilla pod

2 tbsp arrowroot

2 egg yolks

2 tsp clear honey

3 tbsp natural, low-fat *fromage frais*

9 sheets gelatine

1 pineapple, peeled, stalk removed,
   and roughly chopped

4 egg whites

30 g/1 oz/1 cup desiccated
   (shredded) coconut, toasted

30 g/1 oz/¼ cup ground almonds

Garnish

1 quantity honey tuile biscuits (see
   page 144)

cocoa powder, for dusting

edible flowers (e.g. nasturtiums, pot
   marigolds, rose petals, violets)

Serves 4

Put the milk and the vanilla pod into a pan and bring to the boil. Simmer for 5 minutes. Stir a little water into the arrowroot to form a paste, then stir into the milk, mixing in thoroughly. Cook for 1 minute over a moderate heat. Remove the vanilla pod.

In a large mixing bowl, mix the egg yolks and honey together and pour on the warmed, thickened milk, stirring continuously. Pass through a fine sieve into a clean pan and cook over a low heat for 2 minutes, still stirring continuously. Do not boil. Remove from the heat and stir in the *fromage frais*.

Line 4 ramekins with greaseproof (wax) paper; the paper should be 5 cm/2 in higher than the top of each ramekin.

Cover the sheet gelatine with cold water and leave to soften, approximately 5 minutes. Remove from the water with your hand and squeeze out any excess liquid, then place the gelatine in a small heatproof bowl over a pan of barely simmering water. Leave until the gelatine has melted and turned transparent.

Meanwhile, liquidize the pineapple in a liquidizer or food processor and place in a stainless steel saucepan. Bring to the boil and boil for 3 minutes.

When the gelatine has softened, thoroughly stir into the puréed pineapple. Mix with the *fromage frais* custard. Whisk the egg whites until stiff and fold into the mixture. Divide between the ramekins, filling them to the top of the greaseproof (wax) paper. Leave to set in the refrigerator, about three-quarters of an hour.

When the soufflés have set, carefully peel away the paper. Mix the desiccated (shredded) coconut and ground almonds together on a large plate, then dip the soufflés in to coat. To serve, place a soufflé in the centre of each plate, dust with cocoa powder and garnish with flowers and accompany with a honey tuile biscuit.

Fat: high Kcals: 378 Cholesterol: high Fibre: medium

Opposite, from top: Pineapple and Almond Soufflé, and Warm Blueberry Tartlet with Lemon and Cinnamon Ice Cream

Warm Blueberry Tartlets with Lemon and Cinnamon Ice Cream

85 g/3 oz/¾ cup wholemeal flour

25 g/1 oz/⅛ cup raw cane sugar

45 g/1½ oz/¼ cup polyunsaturated margarine

juice of ½ lemon

icing (confectioner's) sugar, for dusting

2 dsp clear honey

2 tsp kirsch

350 g/12 oz/3 cups blueberries

Ice cream

150 ml/5 fl oz/⅔ cup ice cream (see page 143)

2 sticks cinnamon

1 vanilla pod

rind of 1 lemon, grated

Serves 4

Preheat the oven to 180°C/350°F/gas 4. Place a baking sheet in the oven to heat.

Sift the flour and add the sugar and margarine, rubbing in the fat with your fingertips until the mixture resembles coarse breadcrumbs. Add the lemon juice and enough cold water to form a dough. Knead until smooth and place in the refrigerator to rest for 20 minutes.

Roll out the dough on a lightly floured surface to a thickness of 3 mm/⅛ in. Grease 4 × 10 cm/4 in fluted pastry rings and line with the pastry. Bake blind for 5 minutes. Remove from the oven and carefully remove the pastry cases from the rings. Leave to cool on a wire rack. When cool, dust with a little icing (confectioner's) sugar.

Make the basic ice cream mixture but infuse the milk with the cinnamon sticks, vanilla pod and grated lemon rind for 20 minutes.

Warm the honey and kirsch together in a small saucepan. Add the blueberries and cook over a low heat for 3-4 minutes until soft. Spoon a quarter of the fruit into each tartlet and serve with a scoop of ice cream on top; flash under a very hot grill for 15 seconds. Serve immediately.

Fat: high Kcals: 257 Cholesterol: low Fibre: medium

Apple and Berry Strudel

2 cooking apples, grated

1 pinch cinnamon

1 tbsp clear honey

170 g/6 oz/1½ cups mixed berry fruits (e.g. strawberries, raspberries, blueberries)

2 sheets ready-made filo pastry

1 egg white

1 bunch fresh mint, finely chopped

150 ml/5 fl oz/⅔ cup Champneys crème anglaise (see page 142)

Garnish

4 sprigs fresh mint

Serves 4

Preheat the oven to 150°C/300°F/gas 2.

Put the grated apples, cinnamon and 1 teaspoon of the honey in a pan and sweat for 1 minute. Add the mixed berry fruits and cook gently until the fruit is soft, about 6 minutes.

Brush the filo pastry sheets with the egg white and put one sheet on top of the other. Cut the sheets into quarters and place a quarter of the fruit mixture in the centre of each pastry rectangle. Tuck in the ends of the pastry and roll up into a sausage shape.

Brush the pastry rolls with the remaining honey and bake in the oven for 15 minutes until golden brown.

Meanwhile, add the chopped mint to the crème anglaise, stir in well and spoon over the strudel rolls. Garnish with a sprig of mint.

Peach Consommé with Sweet Ravioli

1 vanilla pod
1 star anise
1 stick cinnamon
85 g/3 oz/1¼ cup raw cane sugar
575 ml/1 pt/2½ cups water
4 peaches

Consommé
4 overripe peaches
juice of ½ lemon

Sweet Ravioli
170 g/6 oz sweet pasta (see page 141)
1 tbsp powdered carob
1 pinch saffron powder
20 blackberries
20 raspberries
15 wild strawberries

Garnish
4 sprigs mint

Serves 4

Bring all of the ingredients, except for the peaches, to the boil and simmer for 5 minutes. Add the peaches and poach until they are just cooked. Remove the peaches with a slotted spoon, reserving the poaching liquid for the consommé, and leave to cool. Once the peaches are cool, carefully peel off the skins and put the peaches in the refrigerator.

To make the consommé, boil the peaches in the reserved poaching liquid with the lemon juice until overcooked and mushy. Remove the stones, then strain the liquid through 2 layers of muslin cloth and chill.

To make the sweet ravioli, divide the pasta ingredients into 3. Add the carob powder to one portion, the saffron to another and leave the third plain. Roll out the 3 different pastas as thinly as possible, using a machine or by hand, on one half of each sheet of pasta place 4 piles of 2 of each fruit, then fold over the pasta to enclose the fruit, pressing with your fingers to seal the layers. Set aside a few berries for garnishing and cut round the mounds of fruit with a pastry wheel or large knife to make 3 different shapes. Bring a large pan of water to the boil, drop in the ravioli and cook for 3 minutes until *al dente*. Refresh under cold running water, then place in iced water while you assemble the dish.

To serve, place a poached peach in each bowl, add 3 ravioli and pour over the chilled consommé. Garnish with a sprig of mint and the reserved berries.

Fat: medium Kcals: 297 Cholesterol: high Fibre: high

Peach Consommé with Sweet Ravioli

Iced Carob, Cherry and Pistachio Terrine

55 g/2 oz dark carob
225 g/8 oz light carob
3 sheets gelatine
300 ml/10 fl oz/1¼ cups natural,
    low-fat *fromage frais*
55 g/2 oz pistachio nuts, shelled
115 g/4 oz cherries, stoned and
    halved
115 g/4 oz/1 cup raspberries
flesh of 1 small ripe mango

Garnish
85 g/3 oz/¾ cup raspberries

Melt the dark carob in a *bain marie*. Using a palette knife, spread the melted carob onto a piece of greaseproof (wax) paper to form a rectangle approximately 15 cm × 7 cm/6 in × 3 in. Leave until nearly set, then pull a serrated pastry scraper across the centre to form a wavy line; leave to set. Melt a quarter of the light carob in a *bain marie* and use it to fill in the wavy line. Place in the refrigerator to set fully.

Cover the sheet gelatine with cold water and leave to soften for approximately 5 minutes. Remove from the water with your hand and squeeze out any excess liquid, then place the gelatine in a small heatproof bowl over a pan of barely simmering water. Leave until the gelatine has melted and turned transparent.

Mix together the remaining light carob in a bowl, then stir in the gelatine. Whisk in the *fromage frais*, then add the pistachio nuts and

Iced Carob, Cherry and Pistachio Terrine

85 g/3 oz/¾ cup blackberries
icing (confectioner's) sugar, for
dusting

Serves 8

cherries. Mix in thoroughly and place in a 575 ml/1 pint/2½ cup terrine. Place in the freezer and freeze for 2 hours.

Meanwhile, purée the raspberries in a food processor or liquidizer until smooth, then pass through a muslin cloth. Repeat with the mango, passing the purée through the muslin into a separate bowl.

Cut the carob on the greaseproof (wax) paper into 4 rectangles 4 cm × 7.5 cm/1½ in × 3 in, using a knife dipped in hot water. Peel the rectangles away from the paper and return them to the refrigerator.

To serve, chill 4 dessert plates. Unmould the terrine by turning out onto a plate. Cut into 4 rectangles 4 cm × 7.5 cm/1½ × 3 in. Place a rectangle on each plate, put a slice of carob on top and spoon over the mango purée. Spoon a little raspberry purée around the outside and place a few raspberries in one corner. Garnish with the remaining raspberries and blackberries and dust with a little sugar.

Fat: low Kcals: 143 Cholesterol: low Fibre: medium

Fig, Sultana and Pecan Pie

50 g/2 oz/⅓ cup sultanas

50 ml/2 fl oz/¼ cup dark rum

285 g/10 oz/2½ cups wholemeal flour

140 g/5 oz/¾ cup polyunsaturated spread

juice of ½ lemon

2 tbsp clear honey

200 g/7 oz/1¼ cups dried figs

6 sheets gelatine

55 g/2 oz/⅓ cup pecans, halved

575 ml/1 pt/2½ cups Champneys *crème anglaise* (see page 142)

Serves 10

Soak the sultanas in the rum overnight.

To make the wholemeal pastry, sift the flour into a bowl, then, using the fingertips, rub in the polyunsaturated spread until the mixture resembles breadcrumbs. Sprinkle nearly all the lemon juice and a little water over the mixture and add the honey. Using a round-bladed knife, lightly mix in until the mixture forms large lumps; add a little more water if necessary. Form into a smooth ball, again using the fingertips, then place on a lightly floured surface. Knead until smooth and free of cracks. Form into a ball, wrap in cling film or plastic wrap and leave to rest in the refrigerator for 1 hour.

Grease a 20 cm/10 inch flan ring. On a lightly floured surface, roll out the pastry and use to line the ring. Prick the base of the pastry case, cover and return to the refrigerator for a further 30 minutes.

Preheat the oven to 175°C/325°F/gas 3. Place a baking sheet in the oven to heat.

Place the flan tin on the baking sheet and bake the pastry case blind for 12 minutes. Remove the beans and paper and leave to cool.

Put the figs in a saucepan and just cover with water; add a dash of lemon juice. Put on a lid and simmer for 30 minutes or until the figs are soft. Strain the liquid into a bowl and put the figs to one side. Return the liquid to the saucepan and reduce over a high heat until it forms a light syrup. Set to one side.

Place 3 tablespoons of water in a small heatproof bowl, sprinkle over the gelatine and leave it to go spongy, about 5 minutes. Place the bowl in a saucepan of barely simmering water and leave until the gelatine has melted and turned transparent.

Purée the figs in a blender or food processor. Add the soaked and drained sultanas to the purée, then stir in the melted gelatine. Spoon into the pastry case and place in the refrigerator to set for 1 hour. Once the mixture has set, arrange the pecans attractively on the surface. Reheat the fig syrup until it is warm and spread over the surface to glaze. Allow to cool before serving. Serve with *crème anglaise*.

Fat: high Kcals: 353 Cholesterol: low Fibre: medium

Lemon and Orange Chiffon Pie

170 g/6 oz/1½ cups wholemeal
    flour
2 tbsp low-calorie granulated
    sweetener
85 g/3 oz/⅓ cup polyunsaturated
    spread
juice and zest of 6 oranges and 2
    lemons
3 tsp arrowroot
30 g/1 oz carob
8 egg whites
1 tbsp raw cane sugar
1 tbsp clear honey

Serves 6

Preheat the oven to 220°C/425°F/gas 7.

In a large mixing bowl, rub together the flour, sweetener and polyunsaturated spread and bind with a little water. Roll out the dough on a lightly floured surface and use it to line a 25 cm/10 in flan ring and bake blind. Remove the beams and paper and leave to cool.

Cut the lemon and orange zest into fine strips and add to the lemon and orange juice. Bring to the boil in a small pan. Mix the arrowroot with a little water and add to the juices. Stir to thicken and remove the pan from the heat. When cool, chill in the refrigerator.

Melt the carob in a *bain marie*, spread a thin layer inside the cooled pastry case and chill in the refrigerator. When set, pour in the orange and lemon mixture.

Whisk together the egg whites, sugar and honey until the mixture forms peaks. Spread over the flan and lightly brown under a hot grill.

Fat: high Kcals: 166 Cholesterol: low Fibre: low

Fruit and Nut Slice

100 g/3½ oz/⅓ cup sultanas
75 ml/3 fl oz/⅓ cup rum
5 dried figs
300 ml/10 fl oz/1¼ cups water
14 sheets ready-made filo pastry
1 egg white
75 g/2½ oz/½ cup mixed walnuts
    and hazelnuts, crushed
2 cooking apples, grated
2 ripe bananas, diced (minced)
icing (confectioner's) sugar, for
    dusting

Serves 10

Soak the sultanas in the rum overnight.

Boil the figs in the water for 20 minutes until they form a syrup.

Grease a small baking sheet and place 1 sheet of filo pastry on the base and brush with a little egg white. Sprinkle over a third of the sultanas and cover with another sheet of pastry lightly brushed with egg white. Continue to build up the slice, alternating the pastry with layers of nuts, apple and banana. Finish with a sheet of pastry and again brush with egg white.

Preheat the oven to 150°C/300°F/gas 2.

Pour the fig syrup over the pastry and bake for 20 minutes until golden brown. Remove from the oven and increase the temperature to 180°C/350°F/gas 4.

Slice the pastry into 5 cm/2 in squares, dust with icing (confectioner's) sugar and wrap each square in aluminium foil. Bake for approximately 5 minutes until warmed through. Serve immediately. *Note:* Once the pastry has been wrapped in aluminium foil it can also be cooked over a hot barbecue for 5 minutes.

Fat: medium Kcals: 166 Cholesterol: low Fibre: low

Poached Peaches Served in a Honey Basket with Rosehip Tea and Fig Sorbet

2.25 l/4 pt/10½ cups fresh orange
  juice
2 star anise
4 ripe peaches
55 g/2 oz/¼ cup clear honey
55 g/2 oz/¼ cup raw cane sugar
30 g/1 oz/⅛ cup polyunsaturated
  spread
1 egg white
75 g/2½ oz/½ cup wholemeal flour
8 dried figs
1.1 l/2 pt/5 cups rosehip tea
½ lemon

Garnish
115 g/4 oz/½ cup redcurrants,
  removed from stems, or
  raspberries
icing (confectioner's) sugar, for
  dusting (optional)
4 sprigs mint

Serves 4

Put the orange juice and star anise in a non-stick pan and bring to the boil. Add the peaches and poach in the liquid until tender. Remove from the pan and leave to cool.

Preheat the oven to 220°C/425°F/gas 7.

Using a wooden spoon, mix the honey, sugar and polyunsaturated spread to a smooth paste in a large bowl. Slowly add the egg white and flour, stirring continuously. Spread on a baking sheet in 4 circles, each 10 cm/4 in in diameter, 3 mm/⅛ in thick. Place in the freezer for 5 minutes. Cook in the oven for 4½ minutes then immediately remove from the tray using a spatula or flat knife. Put into a deep, curved mould or rounded tea cup to form a basket shape. Leave to cool.

Boil the figs in the rosehip tea for approximately 10 minutes or until soft. Strain off a quarter of the rosehip tea and reserve. Liquidize the figs with the lemon and a little tea until it is the texture of olive oil. Pass through a sieve into a large bowl. Place in the freezer and whisk vigorously every 20 minutes; it takes about 3 hours for the ice crystals to form. Alternatively place in an ice cream maker or *sorbetière* until stiff. When the sorbet is ready place it in a sealed plastic container in the freezer.

Reduce the reserved tea to a syrup for the sauce. To serve, spoon a pool of tea syrup onto each plate, place a honey basket on top and fill with the sorbet. Add a poached peach to the basket together with small bundles of redcurrants or raspberries. If liked, dust with a little icing (confectioner's) sugar and place a small sprig of mint on top of each peach.

Fat: low Kcals: 357 Cholesterol: low Fibre: high

Opposite: *Poached Peach Served in a Honey Basket with Rosehip Tea and Fig Sorbet*

Mango Charlotte Royale

2 eggs
55 g/2 oz/¼ cup raw cane sugar
55 g/2 oz/½ cup wholemeal flour
1 tbsp reduced sugar strawberry
    preserve

Mousse
2 small, ripe mangos
1 tsp clear honey
8 tsp natural, low-fat *fromage frais*
3 sheets gelatine
115 g/4 oz/1 cup raspberries

Garnish
4 sprigs fresh mint

Serves 4

Preheat the oven to 180°C/350°F/gas 4. Line a Swiss roll tin with greaseproof (wax) paper, then grease the paper.

Put the eggs and sugar in a heatproof bowl, place over a pan of hot water and whisk until almost white. Remove from the heat and fold in the flour using a large metal spoon. Pour the mixture into the lined tin and bake in the oven for 12 minutes until golden. Remove from the oven, turn out of the tin onto a wire rack and leave to cool.

Reserve 2 teaspoons of chopped mango for garnishing the mousse. Remove the stone and liquidize the pulp with the honey and *fromage frais* in a food processor or blender.

Cut the cooled sponge in half lengthways, spread with the strawberry preserve and sandwich the halves together. Cut the sponge into small batons and use to line 4 ramekins.

Add the gelatine to 2 tablespoons of water and leave until it becomes spongy. Melt in a *bain marie* until transparent and stir into the mango mixture. Divide the mixture equally between the ramekins. Place in the refrigerator for 1 hour to set.

Meanwhile, place the raspberries in a food processor or blender and purée. Pass through a fine sieve or muslin cloth.

To serve, plunge the ramekins up to their rims for 30 seconds and turn out onto serving plates, if necessary giving a couple of shakes to loosen. Spoon on the raspberry purée, sprinkle over the diced mango and garnish with sprigs of mint.

Fat: low Kcals: 215 Cholesterol: high Fibre: medium

Poached Peaches with Cinnamon Ice Cream

575 ml/1 pt/2½ cups skimmed milk

1 vanilla pod, seeds removed

1 tsp cornflour or cornstarch mixed
with a little water to form a paste

1 tsp ground cinnamon

2 egg yolks

1 tsp raw cane sugar

4 ripe peaches

575 ml/1 pt/2½ cups fresh orange
juice

50 g/2 oz/⅓ cup fresh raspberries

Garnish

4 sprigs of mint

Serves 4

Place the milk in a pan with the vanilla pod and bring to the boil. Stir in the cornflour or cornstarch paste to thicken, then reduce the heat. Add the cinnamon and simmer, uncovered, for 2 minutes.

In a large clean, dry bowl, beat the egg yolks with the sugar until slightly thickened. Pour over the hot milk, stirring continuously. Place the milk mixture in a clean pan and cook, uncovered, over a low heat for 2 minutes taking care not to boil.

Place the milk in an ice cream maker or *sorbetière* and churn for 15 minutes, or until stiff. Store in a covered container in the freezer. If you do not have an ice cream maker, place the mixture in an un-covered container directly into the freezer. As soon as the mixture has begun to set (about 2 hours), transfer to a chilled mixing bowl and whisk thoroughly until smooth. Return the ice cream to the container and freeze, covered, for approximately 3 hours until stiff.

Place the peaches whole in a non-stick pan with the orange juice, bring to just under boiling point, then cover with a lid and poach for 3 minutes. Transfer the peaches to a plate using a slotted spoon, and as soon as they are cool enough to handle remove and discard the skins. Chill in the refrigerator.

To purée the raspberries, process them in a food processor or blender, then press through a fine sieve. Chill.

About half an hour before serving, transfer the ice cream to the refrigerator so that it will soften slightly and be easy to scoop out. To serve, spoon raspberry purée into the centre of each plate, place a peach on top and surround with quenelles of ice cream. Garnish with sprigs of mint.

Fat: low Kcals: 184 Cholesterol: high Fibre: low

Cherry and Pistachio Carob Terrine

Serves 4

To make the sponge mixture, refer to the recipe for Mango Charlotte Royale (page 132), adding 2 teaspoons of cocoa powder. Line a small square terrine with the mixture.

Make the Carob, Cherry and Pistachio Terrine (see page 126), and 1 quantity of Honey Tuile (see page 144). On removing the tuile from the oven, melt 55 g/2 oz light carob in a *bain marie* and pipe in a spiral. Pull it out with a toothpick or cocktail stick to form a web shape. Cut the tuile into halves and curve into small cone shapes and serve with the terrine.

Fat: high Kcals: 680 Cholesterol: high Fibre: high

Carob Soufflé

55 g/2 oz light carob
150 l/5 fl oz/⅔ cup *crème anglaise*
   (see page 142)
4 sheets gelatine
3 egg whites
3 tbsp natural, low-fat *fromage frais*
2 tbsp carob powder

Serves 4

Melt the carob in a *bain marie* and stir into the *crème anglaise*. Soak the gelatine in cold water for 5 minutes. Remove from the bowl and squeeze out the excess water using your hand. Melt in a heatproof bowl in a *bain marie* and add to the carob mixture. Line 4 small ramekins with greaseproof (wax) paper, leaving a rim 1.5 cm/½ in above the ramekin.

Whisk the egg whites until stiff and fold into the carob mixture, together with the *fromage frais*. Pour into the ramekins and chill in the refrigerator until set, about 30 minutes. When set, remove the greaseproof (wax) paper and roll the edges in carob powder.

Fat: low Kcals: 90 Cholesterol: medium Fibre: low

Carob Tears

225 g/8 oz dark carob, melted in a
   bain marie
5 sheets gelatine
150 ml/5 fl oz/⅔ cup warm *crème
   anglaise* (see page 142)
2 tbsp clear honey
zest of 1 orange, finely diced
   (minced)
3 tbsp Grand Marnier
4 tbsp *crème fraîche*

Cut 4 pieces of greaseproof (wax) paper into rectangles measuring 4 cm × 10 cm/1½ in × 8 in. Using a palette knife, spread a thin layer of melted carob on the paper. When the carob is almost set, stand the rectangles on their sides and curve round into a tear drop shape with the ends touching. Refrigerate for 5 minutes to set firm. Carefully remove the paper and place the carob tears on a flat tray in the freezer.

Cover the sheet gelatine with water and leave for 5 minutes. Remove from the bowl and squeeze out the excess water with your hand. Melt in a heatproof bowl in a *bain marie* until transparent and stir into the warm *crème anglaise*.

Add a little water to the honey, bring to the boil, drop in the orange zest and blanch for 3-4 minutes. Rinse the zest under cold running

Selection of Carob Desserts

Garnish

powdered carob, for dusting

25 g/1 oz/⅓ cup redcurrants or
   raspberries

25 g/1 oz dark carob

Serves 4

water and pat dry on kitchen paper. Add this to the *crème anglaise* together with the Grand Marnier and the *crème fraîche* and chill in the refrigerator. When nearly cool, but still pouring consistency, pour into a carob tear drop shape. Place in the freezer to set, about 30 minutes.

To arrange, place a 10 cm/4 in circular pastry cutter in the centre of each plate and dust the insides with carob powder. Wipe round the cutter, lift from the plate and place a soufflé on top of the powder shape. Melt the dark carob in a *bain marie* and put into a piping bag fitted with a fine nozzle. Pipe elongated fan shapes onto greaseproof (wax) paper. When set, carefully remove from the paper and use to decorate the top of the soufflé. Cut the terrine into 2.5 cm/1 in slices and arrange around the tear drop and soufflé. Add a tuile biscuit cone on one side. Garnish with redcurrants or raspberries.

Fat: medium Kcals: 287 Cholesterol: medium Fibre: medium

Basics
include all the essential dressings, stocks, pasta doughs, sauces, and breads required to produce the delicious meals in this book, as well as supplementing the kitchen cupboard or refrigerator with fresh, tasty supplies.

Basic Vinaigrette

4 tbsp oil (e.g. olive, nut or herb-
   flavoured)
1 tbsp white wine vinegar
sea salt and freshly milled black
   pepper

Makes 6 portions

Mix together all the ingredients until well blended. Store in a sealed container for up to 2 weeks and use as required, mixing well before each serving.

Fat: medium Kcals: 90 Cholesterol: low Fibre: low

Tomato Vinaigrette

1 tbsp white wine vinegar
4 tbsp extra virgin olive oil
5 large, overripe tomatoes
sea salt and freshly milled black
   pepper

Makes 6 portions

Place the vinegar, oil and tomatoes in a food processor or liquidizer and process for 2–3 minutes until the mixture reaches a coating consistency. Season to taste with salt and black pepper. Pass through a muslin cloth into a clean container. Seal and store in the refrigerator for up to 3 days, using as required.

Fat: high Kcals: 111 Cholesterol: low Fibre: low

Cucumber and Ginger Vinaigrette

½ cucumber
2 tbsp extra virgin olive oil
2 tbsp white wine vinegar
½ tsp fresh ginger, peeled and
   finely chopped
sea salt and freshly milled black
   pepper

Makes 6 portions

Combine all the ingredients in a liquidizer or food processor. Blend vigorously, then press through a fine sieve or muslin cloth. It will keep in a sealed container in the refrigerator for up to 1 week.

Fat: medium Kcals: 48 Cholesterol: low Fibre: low

Orange and Basil Dressing

575 ml/1 pt/2½ cups fresh orange
   juice
1 medium-sized potato, peeled and
   diced (minced)
1 sprig basil

Makes 6 portions

Place the orange juice and the potato in a pan and cook over a high heat until the potato is cooked and the orange juice reduced by half.

Pour the reduced juice and the potato into a food processor or blender, add the basil and process for 1 minute. Pass the dressing through a muslin cloth and store in the refrigerator in an airtight container for up to 1 week. Use as required.

Fat: low Kcals: 49 Cholesterol: low Fibre: low

Strawberry Vinaigrette

6 strawberries
1 tbsp balsamic vinegar
3 tbsp walnut oil
sea salt and freshly milled black
   pepper

Makes 6 portions

Purée the strawberries in a food processor or blender, then pass them through a muslin cloth. Clean the blender or processor and return the strawberry liquor to the blender container. Gently stir in the balsamic vinegar and add the walnut oil at slow speed until it is fully blended with the strawberry juices. Season to taste.

Store in the refrigerator in a sealed container and use as required. Shake well before use.

Fat: medium Kcals: 72 Cholesterol: low Fibre: low

Tomato Concasse – Raw

Prepare quantities as required using
   large, ripe tomatoes

Cut each tomato into quarters, discard the seeds and excess pulp. Using a very sharp knife, carefully remove the skin from each tomato quarter. Finely chop each quarter into small dice.

Tomato Concasse – Cooked

15 large, ripe tomatoes
2 small onions, finely chopped
1 tbsp olive oil
1 tbsp white wine
1 tsp fresh mixed herbs (e.g.
    tarragon, thyme, basil and
    coriander), finely chopped

Makes approximately 6 portions

Proceed as for raw tomato concasse.

Sweat the onions in a frying pan (skillet) in the olive oil until translucent. Deglaze with 1 tablespoon of white wine, then add the tomato concasse and cook over a medium heat until soft. Add finely chopped mixed herbs as desired.

Fat: low Kcals: 94 Cholesterol: low Fibre: medium

Chicken Stock

1.35 kg/3 lb chicken carcasses
3.5 l/6 pt/15 cups cold water
2 medium-sized carrots
1 head celery
2 medium-sized leeks
3 medium-sized onions
1 bay leaf

Makes 1.75 litres/3 pints/7½ cups

Preheat the oven to 220°C/425°F/gas 7.

Roast the chicken carcasses in the oven for 20 minutes until lightly browned. When browned, place the carcasses in a deep pan and just cover with water. Roughly chop the vegetables and add them to the pan with the bay leaf. Bring to the boil, skimming the surface to remove any scum. Cover and simmer for approximately 2 hours, skimming the surface when necessary until the liquid is reduced by half.

Pass the stock through a fine sieve and discard the bones and vegetables. Leave the stock to cool, then refrigerate. Remove the fat from the surface before use. The stock can be kept for up to 3 days in the refrigerator and for up to 3 months if frozen.

Fat: low Kcals: 35 Cholesterol: low Fibre: low

Fish stock

900 g/2 lb fish bones (e.g. plaice,
    large sole, brill)
1 large leek
1 bulb fennel
1 large onion
1 lemon
3 sprigs parsley
6 white peppercorns
1.1 l/2 pints/5 cups water

Makes 1.1 litres/2 pints/5 cups

Place the fish bones in a pan, cover and sweat for 2–3 minutes to release the juices.

Slice the leek, fennel and onion and add to the fish bones together with all the other ingredients. Cover with 1.1 litres/2 pints/5 cups cold water, bring to the boil and simmer for 20 minutes, skimming the surface as necessary. Pass the stock through a fine sieve and discard the bones and vegetables. Leave to cool and store in a sealed container in the refrigerator for up to 3 days.

Fat: low Kcals: 35 Cholesterol: low Fibre: low

Vegetable Stock

2 large courgettes (zucchini)
4 large onions
1 bulb fennel
115 g/4 oz/½ cup celeriac
2 medium-sized leeks
2 large carrots, peeled
1 head celery
6 cloves garlic
1 tbsp olive oil
1.75 l/3 pt/7½ cups cold water
1 bunch fresh chervil
1 bunch fresh basil
1 bunch fresh thyme
1 star anise

Makes 1.75 litres/3 pints/7½ cups

Finely chop all the vegetables and the garlic. Heat the olive oil in a pan and sweat the vegetables until the onion is translucent. Add the cold water and bring to the boil, then cover and simmer for 10 minutes. Finely chop the herbs and add to the vegetable mixture together with the star anise. Simmer for a further 2 minutes. Pass through a fine sieve, discard the vegetables and leave the stock to cool.

Place the stock in an airtight container and use as required. The stock will keep for up to 3 days in the refrigerator and up to 3 months if frozen.

Fat: low Kcals: 35 Cholesterol: low Fibre: low

Veal Stock

450 g/1 lb veal bones
2 carrots, roughly chopped
1 head celery, roughly chopped
3 onions, roughly chopped
2 leeks, roughly chopped
3.5 l/6 pt/15 cups cold water
1 bouquet garni

Makes 1.75 l/3 pints/7½ cups

Preheat the oven to 220°C/425°F/gas 7.

Place the veal bones in a roasting tray and roast for 25 minutes until lightly browned. Place the roughly chopped vegetables in a deep pan and soften for approximately 15 minutes over a medium heat. Add the browned bones to the vegetables and cover with cold water. Bring to the boil, skimming off the excess fat as necessary. Add the bouquet garni, cover and simmer for 2-3 hours. Then reduce the liquid over a high heat by half.

Pass the stock through a fine sieve and discard the bones and vegetables. Leave to cool and store in an airtight container. The stock can be kept for up to 3 days in the refrigerator and up to 3 months if frozen.

Fat: low Kcals: 35 Cholesterol: low Fibre: low

Peach and Lemon Chutney

500 g/8 oz/1 cup dried peaches
500 ml/16 fl oz/2 cups water
juice and grated zest of 6 lemons
200 ml/7 fl oz/¾ cup cider vinegar
400 ml/14 fl oz/1¾ cups
   concentrated apple juice
2 cloves garlic
2 large green chillies
1½ tsp coriander seeds
1 tsp ground cardomom
½ tsp ground cloves
100 g/3½ oz/½ cup currants
2 apples, peeled and quartered

Makes 900 g/2 lb

Slice the peaches and soak them overnight in the water in a pan.

The next day, add the grated rind from the lemons, the lemon juice, vinegar and apple juice to the soaked fruit. Simmer, uncovered, until the peaches are soft, approximately 45 minutes, stirring gently from time to time to prevent the peaches from sticking to the pan.

Finely chop the garlic and green chillies in a food processor or blender and add to the pan together with all remaining ingredients.

Bring the mixture to the boil, cover, and reduce the heat and simmer gently for approximately 25 minutes until the apples lose their pale colour, the currants plump up and the chutney thickens. Stir occasionally to prevent sticking.

While the mixture is cooking, sterilize as many heatproof screw-top glass jars as are required for the quantity of chutney made. Wash the jars and their lids in water and detergent and then boil in water for 10 minutes. Dry upside down in a warm oven.

Allow the chutney to cool and store in the sterilized glass jars in the refrigerator for up to 1 month. The flavour improves considerably after a couple of weeks.

Fat: medium Kcals total: 2065 Cholesterol: low Fibre: high

Wholemeal Pasta

2 egg whites
150 ml/5 fl oz/⅔ cup water
100 g/3½ oz/¾ cup plain flour
200 g/7 oz/1¾ cups wholemeal
   flour
1 pinch salt
½ tsp truffle oil
½ tsp hazelnut oil

Makes 300 g/10½ oz dough

Whisk the egg whites and water together until well blended. Sift the plain and wholemeal flours and the salt together. Make a well in the centre and add the oils to it; stir in thoroughly. Slowly add the egg mixture to the flour and mix to a smooth dough, either by hand or in a food processor or blender.

On a lightly floured board, knead the dough until firm with the heel of your hand. The dough should be firm and elastic; if it is too sticky add a little more flour.

Roll out the pasta on a lightly floured surface until the pasta is 2 mm/⅛ in thick. Alternatively, pass through a pasta machine for a more even finish.

Cook for 3–4 minutes in salted boiling water until *al dente*. Drain and serve immediately.

Fat: high Kcals total: 1035 Cholesterol: low Fibre: high

Saffron Pasta

To add extra flavour and yellow colour to pasta soak 1 teaspoon of powdered saffron in 25 ml/1½ tablespoons of warm water for 20 minutes. Add the saffron infusion to 1 quantity of Wholemeal Pasta dough at the same time as the oils.

Spinach Pasta

To add green colour and a stronger flavour to pasta, add 55 g/2 oz/1½ cups of chopped fresh spinach to 1 quantity of Wholemeal Pasta mixture. Mix well, either by hand or in a food processor or blender until a smooth dough is formed. If the mixture seems dry, slowly add up to 3 tablespoons of cold water.

Fat: high Kcals (total): 1035 Cholesterol: low Fibre: high

Sweet Pasta

110 g/4 oz/1 cup flour, plain or
   wholemeal
1 small egg
2 tsp low-calorie granulated
   sweetener
1 dsp extra virgin olive oil

Makes 150 g/5½ oz dough

Mix all the ingredients in a food processor or blender for 1 minute. On a lightly floured surface knead to form an elastic dough. Leave to rest in the refrigerator for 1 hour before rolling as for Wholemeal Pasta.

Fat: high Kcals (total): 508 Cholesterol: high Fibre: high

Champneys Bechamel

575 ml/1 pt/2½ cups skimmed milk
1 small button onion
1 bay leaf
2 cloves garlic
25 g/1 oz/⅛ cup cornflour or
   cornstarch, mixed with a little
   water to form a paste

Makes 575 ml/1 pint/2½ cups

Pour the milk into a pan and add the onion, bay leaf and garlic cloves. Slowly bring to the boil, then simmer for 5 minutes. Remove and discard the onion, bay leaf and garlic and return the milk to the boil. When boiling, stir in the cornflour or cornstarch paste and continue stirring until the mixture reaches coating consistency. Cook for a further 2 minutes, then press through a fine sieve.

Fat: low Kcals: 293 Cholesterol: low Fibre: low

Champneys Muesli

575 ml/1 pt/2½ cups natural, low-
　　fat yoghurt (see page 142)
2 dsp sultanas
1 tbsp chopped mixed nuts
3 dsp jumbo oats
1 dsp clear honey
1 large, ripe banana
115 g/4 oz/1 cup mixed berry fruits
2 red apples, grated
1 green apple, grated

Garnish
1 dsp toasted oats
1 bunch mint

Serves 6

In a large bowl, mix together thoroughly all the ingredients except the banana, berry fruits and apples. Leave the mixture overnight in the refrigerator.

Before serving, slice the banana and any large berry fruits and grate the apples, including the peel, and add to the mixture. Stir well and garnish with toasted oats and mint leaves.

Fat: low Kcals: 155 Cholesterol: low Fibre: low

Yoghurt

575 ml/1 pt/2½ cups skimmed milk
2 tsp skimmed milk powder
2 tsp live natural low-fat yoghurt

Makes 575 ml/1 pint/2½ cups

Ensure that all the utensils are clean, otherwise contamination may occur. Put all the ingredients in a small saucepan. Heat to blood temperature, 37°C/96°F. Pour into a sterilized thermos or vacuum flask. Leave for 10 hours with the lid on. Refrigerate and serve.

Fat: low Kcals: 230 Cholesterol: low Fibre: low

Champneys Crème Anglaise

575 ml/1 pt/2½ cups skimmed milk
1 vanilla pod
1 tsp arrowroot, mixed with a little
　　water to form a paste
3 egg yolks
2 tbsp low-calorie granulated
　　sweetener

Makes 575 ml/1 pint/2½ cups

Gently heat the milk and vanilla pod together for about 5 minutes, bring to the boil and add the arrowroot paste, stirring until slightly thickened. Cook for 2 minutes on a medium heat. Leave to cool.

Place the egg yolks and sweetener in a large mixing bowl and whisk until thick and white, 3–4 minutes. Whisk in the milk, and when thoroughly blended transfer to a clean pan and gently reheat, stirring constantly. Do not allow the custard to boil or it will curdle. Remove the vanilla pod and pass the custard through a fine sieve. It is now ready to serve but will keep for up to 3 days in the refrigerator.

Fat: high Kcals: 470 Cholesterol: high Fibre: low

Ice Cream

300 ml/10 fl oz/1¼ cups milk

1 vanilla pod

2 tsp egg replacer

1 tsp water

4 tbsp low-calorie granulated
sweetener

1 tsp cornflour or cornstarch, mixed
with a little water to form a paste

2 tsp *crème fraîche*

Serves 4

Pour the milk into a saucepan, add the vanilla pod and bring to the boil. Meanwhile, in a large bowl, lightly whip the egg replacer in 1 teaspoon of water. Add the sweetener and whisk until smooth.

Put the cornflour or cornstarch paste into another large bowl. As soon as the milk comes to the boil, remove from the heat, discard the vanilla pod and pour the milk onto the paste, stirring continuously, to thicken. Return the milk to the pan and simmer for 2–3 minutes to blend thoroughly, stirring from time to time. Pour the thickened milk onto the egg mixture, whisking with a fork as you pour. Leave until cool and fold in the *crème fraîche*. Pour the mixture through a fine sieve into a mixing bowl. Place in the freezer and whisk vigorously every 20 minutes (use an electric hand–whisk or a rotary whist) until the ice cream is set, about 4–5 hours. Alternatively, place the mixture in an ice cream maker or *sorbetière* and churn until firm.

When the ice cream has set, place in a freezer container with an airtight lid and use as required. The ice cream will keep in the freezer for up to 1 week.

Fat: low Kcals: 88 Cholesterol: low Fibre: low

Basic Bread

250 ml/8 fl oz/1 cup lukewarm
water

30 g/1 oz/2 cakes fresh yeast

500 g/1 lb 2 oz/4½ cups strong
plain flour

1 tbsp salt

1 tbsp skimmed milk powder

20 g/¾ oz/1 tsp polyunsaturated
spread

Makes a 900 g/2 lb loaf, or 16 rolls

Put half the water in a small bowl, stir in the yeast and leave to ferment and froth, 5–8 minutes. Sift all the dry ingredients into a large mixing bowl, then mix in the polyunsaturated spread, using your fingertips, until the mixture resembles breadcrumbs. Make a well in the centre and add the remaining water and yeast. Mix in well, using your hand, then knead to form a soft dough, 5–8 minutes. Leave to rise for 30 minutes in a warm place, then lightly knead again for about 1 minute to knock the dough back to its original size. Leave to rise for another 30 minutes, then divide into the required portions and place on grease-proof (wax) paper on a baking sheet. Leave to prove for 15 minutes.

Preheat the oven to 190°C/375°F/gas 5.

Bake in the oven for 30 minutes until the bread is well browned and crisp on all sides. If the bread is done, it should sound hollow when tapped on the base. Transfer to a wire rack and leave to cool.

Fat: low Kcals: 119 Cholesterol: low Fibre: low

Wholemeal Pastry

115 g/4 oz/1 cup wholemeal flour
1 pinch of sea salt
55 g/2 oz/¼ cup polyunsaturated
    margarine
50-75 ml/2-3 fl oz/¼-⅓ cup water

Makes 1 quantity for 20 cm/8 in
    flan dish

Sift the flour and a pinch of salt together. Using a fork, break up the margarine in the flour and salt to achieve a crumbly texture. Mix in the water until a soft dough is formed and leave the pastry to rest in a covered container in the refrigerator. Roll out the pastry as required and use to line a greased or non-stick 20 cm/8 in circular quiche or flan dish.

Fat: high Kcals (total): 887 Cholesterol: low Fibre: high

Wholemeal Cinnamon Muffins

200 g/7 oz/1¾ cups wholemeal
    flour
3 tsp ground cinnamon
25 g/1 oz/⅛ cup baking powder
45 g/1½ oz/¼ cup raw cane sugar
45 g/1½ oz/¼ cup polyunsaturated
    spread
2 eggs
250 ml/8 fl oz/1 cup skimmed milk
icing (confectioner's) sugar, for
    sprinkling

Makes 12 muffins

Preheat the oven to 205°C/400°F/gas 6. Place a baking sheet in the oven to hear.

Sift the flour, cinnamon and baking powder into a mixing bowl. Add the sugar and the polyunsaturated spread and, using your finger-tips, rub in well to form fine crumbs. Make a well in the centre of the flour. Gradually add the eggs and milk, mixing in with a knife to form a smooth paste; the mixture should be of dropping consistency.

Grease 12 muffin tins liberally with polyunsaturated spread. Spoon the dough a quarter of the way up each tin (the dough will rise when cooking) and bake in the oven for 15–20 minutes, until well risen and golden brown. Place on a wire rack to cool.

To serve, sprinkle with icing (confectioner's) sugar.

Fat: low Kcals: 125 Cholesterol: medium Fibre: low

Honey Tuile

30 g/1 oz/¼ cup clear honey
55 g/2 oz/¼ cup raw cane sugar
1½ oz polyunsaturated fat
85 g/3 oz/¾ cup wholemeal flour
1 egg white

Makes 20 biscuits or 10 baskets

Mix the honey, sugar and polyunsaturated fat to a smooth paste using a wooden spoon. Fold in the flour and egg white a little at a time, again to form a smooth paste. The paste should be of dropping consistency. Place in a clean bowl, cover the top of the bowl with cling film or plastic wrap and use as required, storing in the refrigerator for up to 2 days.

Fat: low Kcals: 46 Cholesterol: low Fibre: low

Champneys Fruit Loaf

140 g/5 oz/1¼ cups self-raising
   flour

140 g/5 oz/1¼ cups wholemeal
   self-raising flour

¼ tsp salt

½ tsp baking powder

200 g/7 oz/1¼ cups dark
   muscovado sugar

55 g/2 oz/½ cup skimmed
   milk powder

30 g/1 oz/¼ cup wheatgerm

55 g/2 oz/⅓ cup raisins

45 g/1½ oz/⅓ cup dried apricots,
   chopped

30 g/1 oz/¼ cup walnuts, chopped

30 g/1 oz/¼ cup hazelnuts,
   chopped

3 eggs

175 ml/6 fl oz/¾ cup fresh orange
   juice

75 ml/3 fl oz/⅓ cup olive oil

1 banana, diced (minced)

Serves 12

Preheat the oven to 175°C/325° F/gas 3. Grease a 450 g/1 lb loaf tin and line with greaseproof (wax) paper.

Mix all the dry ingredients together including the nuts and dried fruit. In a separate bowl, whisk together the eggs, orange juice, oil and bananas until frothy. Make a well in the centre of the dry ingredients and add the banana mixture, stirring until mixed. Spoon into the prepared tins and bake for about 1 hour until the loaf pulls from the sides of the tin and a skewer inserted in the centre comes out clean.

When cooked, remove from the tin and cool on a wire rack before wrapping in greaseproof (wax) paper and storing in an airtight tin for up to a week.

Fat: high Kcals: 313 Cholesterol: medium Fibre: low

Sultana, Walnut and Banana Bread

3 ripe bananas

55 g/2 oz/¼ cup polyunsaturated
   spread

1 egg, beaten

zest of 1 orange, grated

255 g/9 oz/6¼ cups wholemeal
   flour

1 pinch baking powder

1 pinch salt

45 g/1½ oz/⅓ cup chopped
   walnuts

55 g/2 oz/¼ cup sultanas, soaked
   in cold water for 4 hours

4 tbsp low-calorie granulated
   sweetener

Preheat the oven to 180°C/350°F/gas 4. Place a baking sheet in the oven to heat.

Mash the bananas with a fork and beat in the polyunsaturated spread. Stir in the beaten egg and grated orange zest. Sieve the flour, baking powder and salt into a separate mixing bowl. Add the walnuts, sultanas and sweetener and make a well in the centre. Pour in the banana mixture and beat until smooth using a wooden spoon.

Line a 450 g/1 lb loaf tin with lightly oiled greaseproof (wax) paper. Pour the mixture into the tin, place on the baking sheet and bake for 1 hour until golden brown. Turn out onto a wire rack. Serve sliced and spread with a thin layer of polyunsaturated spread.

Fat: high Kcals (total): 2146 Cholesterol: high Fibre: high

Menus

January (Family Dinner)

A Salad of Marinated Pigeon with Walnuts and Grapes

Cod Baked with Wild Mushrooms, Tarragon and White Wine

Bread and Fruit Pudding with Banana Sauce

Above; *A Family Dinner in January;* opposite: *February's St Valentine's Day meal*

February (St Valentine's Day)

Scallop, Bacon and Mushroom Salad with Maple Dressing

Roasted Fillet of Pork with Apricot and Onion

Mango Charlotte Royale

March (Light Buffet)

Wild Mushroom and Lentil Salad

Red Mullet with Salad Niçoise

Apricot, Fig and Coconut Terrine

April (Anniversary Lunch)

Vegetable and Nut Croquettes

Stuffed Breast of Corn Chicken with a Tomato Vinaigrette

A Tulip of Passion Fruit and Apricot Sorbet with Fresh Fruits

May (Birthday Lunch)

Wild Mushroom and Chicken Terrine

Red Mullet with Salad Niçoise

Lemon and Orange Chiffon Pie

June (Barbecue)

Avocado and Sweetcorn Soup

Barbecued Chicken Chilli and Pineapple Wrapped in a Cornflour Pasty

Fruit and Nut Slice

July (Garden Party)

Champneys Gazpacho

Salmon Poached in Champagne Served with Cucumber and Watercress Salad

Warm Blueberry Tartlets with Lemon and Cinnamon Ice Cream

August (Light Lunch)

Melon Lime Soup

Celeriac and Wild Mushroom Terrine

Poached Peach with Cinnamon Ice Cream

September (Celebration Supper)

Sardine and Red Onion Terrine

Quail with Sweet Pepper Sauce and Autumn Vegetables

Champneys Apple Crumble with Honey-Sweetened Fromage Frais

October (Dinner Party)

Chicken Leek Mousse with Beetroot Salad

Roasted Fillet of Veal with Roasted Shallots and Garlic with a Madeira Sauce

Kiwi and Orange Slice with Sweet Vinaigrette

November (After Theatre Meal)

Mexican Bean Soup

Smoked Gammon Brochette with Celeriac and Apple Cakes

Banana en Papillote

December (Christmas Day)

Scallops Poached in Caraway and Saffron

Pheasant and Quail Stuffed with Apple and Cranberry Forcemeat

Apricot and Passion Fruit Water Ice

Fig, Sultana and Pecan Pie

Above: *A Light Lunch in August;* opposite: *December's Christmas Day feast*

Glossary

Al dente – an Italian term used to indicate the point at which food is perfectly cooked. It is usually used with reference to pasta which should be soft but still chewy when ready. The cooking time varies according to the type and shape of pasta used but with a little experimentation judging the *al dente* point becomes easy.

Alfalfa sprouts – these grains can be sprouted within a week. Choose whole grains free of chemicals that are sold for cooking rather than sowing. To prepare, soak overnight in warm water. Drain and place in a sterilized glass container, large enough to hold the sprouts which will expand to 5 or 6 times their original size. Cover with a small cotton or muslin square and place in a warm place, out of direct sunlight. Rinse 2 or 3 times with fresh water every day until fully sprouted. To use, drain and discard any unsprouted grains.

Arrowroot – an effective powder thickener of liquids and sauces. To avoid lumps mix to a paste with a little water before adding to the mixture to be thickened. After adding to the liquid stir in well, usually over heat.

Bain marie – cooking in a *bain marie* allows gentle and even heat distribution in the preparation of dishes using delicate ingredients which are better cooked away from direct heat or flame (e.g. sauces, carob or chocolate, and gelatine). To set up a *bain marie*, bring a large pan of water to the boil. Put a heat proof bowl or smaller pan into the first pan, resting on the boiling water. Lower the heat slightly, add the ingredients to the smaller container and simmer until cooked or melted. Make sure the larger pan does not boil dry.

Baking blind – this method of baking pastry is used where a tart of flan case needs to be partially or fully cooked for crispness before a filling is added. Roll out the pastry and use to line a flan or pie tin. Cover with greaseproof (wax) paper, leaving a small rim extending above the top of the tin. Fill the pastry case with uncooked rice, dried beans

or ceramic baking 'beans' (sold at most specialist kitchen shops). To partially cook, bake for about 5 minutes in a moderate-hot oven until the pastry is golden. To cook fully, leave in the oven for approximately 15 minutes until brown. Remove the rice or beans and paper and leave to cool in the tin, then transfer to a wire rack.

Blanching – the blanching method used in these recipes refers to parboiling by blanching where ingredients are plunged into boiling water for 1 or 2 minutes (longer if specified in the recipe). This retains colour in vegetables and helps to preserve various nutrients. The food items are then usually 'refreshed' under iced or cold water to stop any further cooking from taking place.

Borage – both the leaves and small deep blue flowers of this herb are edible and can be used in salads or for garnishing. If using the leaves, pick them when young before the hairy covering thickens.

Bouquet garni – a selection of herbs, fresh or dried, which always includes thyme, bay leaf and parsley, and any others according to taste. The sprigs are tied into a bundle using string or wrapped in a small piece of muslin. The bouquet garni should be removed before serving.

Cardomom pod (bean) – this spice pod is available in 2 varieties, 'green' or white, and black. The black pods are milder and are often used in Indian dishes. For the best flavour, buy cardomom in pod rather than powder form.

Carob – similar to chocolate, carob is produced from the carob or locust bean. It is available in bars, chips or powder. Carob is lower in fat than chocolate and contains no caffeine.

Caul fat – this is the fatty membrane that lines a pig's stomach. It is often used for wrapping meat and meat terrines; it helps prevent the meat from drying out.

Chinois – a fine stainless steel sieve which allows for effective straining of liquids.

Charlotte – a custard- or cream-based dessert made in a traditional tall mould. A 'Charlotte Royale' is supported by a layer of sponge around the sides and base of the mould.

Coating consistency – a sauce of coating consistency should be thick enough to coat food evenly. To test for this, put a wooden spoon into the sauce and draw a finger across the back of the spoon. If the sauce is ready a clearly defined trail should be left.

Concasse – from the French verb *concasser*, to chop coarsely; a concasse is a dish of coarsely chopped vegetables, usually tomatoes.

Coulibiac – a layered fish dish surrounded in pastry, originating from Russia.

Crème anglaise – a light vanilla custard (see page 142).

Crème fraîche – a French cultured cream similar to soured cream. The minimum fat content of 29 per cent means that it will not separate quickly on heating. To make *crème fraîche*, use double (heavy) cream mixed with half its volume of soured cream or yoghurt. Warm the two together but do not boil. Remove from the heat, put in a clean bowl, cover with a cloth and keep in a warm place for approximately 8 hours. Then store in the fridge.

Dropping consistency – when a sauce or mixture reaches this point it should be thick enough to drip rather than pour off a wooden spoon. If the drops are allowed to fall onto a clean, flat surface they should retain their shape without flowing outwards.

Filo pastry – extremely thin sheets of pastry made from flour and water, used extensively in Greek, Turkish and Middle Eastern cooking. Buy ready-made fresh or frozen sheets of pastry. To use, brush with olive oil, or egg white for fewer calories.

Fromage frais – this unripened cheese resembles thick yoghurt. It has a very low fat content, ranging from 0 to 8 per cent. Higher fat varieties are available but the lower fat types are very useful as a replacement for cream in low-fat recipes. *Fromage frais* can be served cold in the same way as yoghurt, or in hot dishes. However, take care not to overheat or it will separate and form lumps.

Galantine – a dish of stuffed and rolled white meat served cold in jelly.

Garlic oil – this is olive oil infused with cloves of garlic to give it extra flavour. To make garlic oil, peel several cloves of garlic and place in a clean glass jar. Fill the jar with olive oil. Cover and leave to infuse for about 10 days. Use as required.

Gelatine – this is available in both powder and sheet form and is used to set dishes that are moulded or that require extra setting properties. Both types of gelatine are soaked in cold water to form a gel and are then melted to a transparent liquid in a *bain marie*. Stir well on adding the gelatine to the other ingredients to ensure even distribution. Do not attempt to add gelatine to a dish containing raw pineapple as the fruit's natural enzymes will prevent setting.

Ice cream maker or sorbetière – this machine stirs the ice cream or sorbet mixture while keeping it at a temperature below freezing point. Invaluable for regular ice cream making in large quantities, an ice cream maker reduces the amount of manual stirring that is otherwise needed.

Kumquat – this orange-coloured fruit is the smallest of the citrus family. It has a distinctive bittersweet flavour and both the skin and the flesh can be eaten raw, poached, candied, sliced with meat or in salads, stewed as a sauce or pickled.

Larder trimmed – to have all fat and sinew removed from a cut of meat.

Lardons – small 6 mm/⅛ in strips cut from bacon rashers, with the rind removed. Some shops sell ready-cut lardons; to cut at home, simply chop the rashers into strips, layer them on top of each other and cut again until you reach the required size.

Lentils: *puy* – these small dark green lentils are grown in the Le Puy area of France. They have a very good flavour and hold their shape during cooking.

Madeira – a fortified wine from Spain, often used in sauces. It is available in dry or sweet varieties.

Maple syrup – a sweet syrup made from the boiled sap of the maple tree. It is available in two grades: Number 1 is thinner and easier to pour and is best used as a sauce over ice cream, pancakes or waffles; Number 2 is thicker and is better for cooking. Once opened, store the syrup in the refrigerator. Be careful not to confuse maple syrup with maple-flavoured syrup, a synthetic substitute with an inferior flavour.

Mushrooms – wild mushrooms of various types are now increasingly available in shops. Two particularly delicious types are morels and chanterelles (which include girolles and horns of plenty). Morels have curiously corrugated caps and should be soaked in cold water for 5 minutes before cooking to remove any dirt or insects. Rinse under running water and drain on kitchen paper.

Girolle mushrooms are yellow in colour with slightly ragged edges, while horns of plenty are dark brown with a hollow trumpet-shaped centre; both need only a quick wipe before cooking. They can be baked, stewed or stir-fried. Both morels and chanterelles are available dried.

Note: Unless you are an expert in mushroom identification it is not advisable to gather your own crop in the countryside; many varieties of wild mushroom are highly poisonous.

Muslin cloth – a porous fine cotton cloth which is ideal for straining liquids, some fruit purées and cheese-making.

Mussels – to prepare for cooking, scrub the shells under cold running water and remove any barnacles or weeds. Throw out any with broken shells or which do not shut when knocked gently with a knife. Cut away the beard strings. To cook, follow instructions given in the recipes.

Oil: *olive* – this is a versatile oil high in monounsaturated fat made from pressing olives. Olive oil comes in various grades: the most popular are 'extra virgin', . made at the first pressing, with a stronger flavour, and the cheaper standard olive oil which is milder in taste. Olive oil is multi-purpose and can be used for shallow-frying, in salad dressings, even in baking dough.

Peanut (also known as groundnut oil) – this is a light oil with a mild flavour. It is used for frying and in salad dressings where the stronger flavour of olive oil is less suitable.

Sesame – French sesame oil and Asian toasted sesame oil are both produced from sesame seeds, yet the former is pressed from the raw seeds. The toasted seed oil has a richer taste and should be used in small quantities; it is normally added at the end of the cooking time.

Hazelnut and walnut oils – these oils are pressed from the nuts and have a very distinctive aromatic flavour. Do not heat excessively or the flavour will be considerably diminished.

Truffle oil – this is olive or sunflower oil infused with truffles; a real luxury – use sparingly.

Parma ham – ham cured using the traditional processes of the town of Parma in northern Italy. It should be served in paper-thin slices with the fatty edges removed.

Pasta machine – this machine rolls pasta dough to ever-decreasing thicknesses. Many machines have different settings or attachments for producing a variety of widths and types of strip or shape.

Provençale – a style of cooking combining garlic, tomatoes and olive oil originating from the Provence region of southern France.

Proving dough – leaving yeasted dough to rise or prove before baking, ideally in a warm place, allows fermentation to take place.

Polyunsaturated spread – a margarine made from soya or sunflower oils which are low in saturated fats and high in polyunsaturated fats. Spreads made from olive oil have similar uses and are equally suitable for greasing, baking and using in some sauces.

Quail's eggs – these tiny speckled eggs can be found in specialist stores. They are usually served hard-boiled (5 minutes) and are often presented with their shells on for visual effect.

Quenelles – these are elongated spheres made from raw fish or white poultry meat, mixed with eggs and often other ingredients for flavour or added binding qualities. Once moulded, quenelles are quickly cooked in simmering water and can be served with a sauce or in soup.

Rice: *Brown* – rice grains with the husk left on. These are chewy and have extra fibre. Brown rice takes about 40 minutes to cook but can take less time if soaked overnight.

Wild – this grain grows in lakes in North America. Although part of the crop is now cultivated, some of the harvest is still hand-picked from the wild plants. Black and shiny in appearance, the grains are boiled for approximately 40 minutes until chewy.

Ramekin – a small, round, ovenproof dish for making individual soufflés or moulds.

Refreshing – see Blanching

Saffron – the world's most expensive spice, saffron consists of the hand-picked stamens of the saffron crocus. Its distinctive flavour is brought out well in rice dishes, sweet cakes and breads and with fish. Saffron is available in either thread or powder form. To use the threads, infuse in a small amount of warm water before adding to the dish.

Sake – a Japanese wine with a high alcohol content, produced from fermented rice. It can be added to food or drunk on its own, when it is traditionally served hot.

Stir-frying – this method of frying, usually in a wok or deep frying pan (skillet) is very quick and seals in the flavour of the food as well as using the minimum of fat. To stir-fry small pieces of meat or vegetables, heat a small amount of oil in a wok until it is smoking. Add the ingredients and keep them moving by stirring them around the pan.

Sorbetière – see Ice cream maker

Tahini paste – a strongly flavoured paste made from crushed, toasted sesame seeds. The seeds and the oil tend to separate in the jar so shake well before use.

Terrine – a straight-sided ovenproof dish, usually lidded. The shape and size can vary. Small pâté terrines provide individual portions while the larger 1.1 litre/2 pint/5 cup dishes serve up to 14.

Timbale – a small moulded mound of meat, fish or vegetables, named after the ceramic dish of the same name.

Vinegar: *Red or white wine* – as the name suggests, these are made from wine; they are most commonly used in salad dressings.

Cider – this is derived from cider and is useful for preserving and pickling, although it can also be drunk on its own, diluted with water.

Balsamic – an Italian vinegar produced from grapes in a traditional and lengthy process of fermentation, often taking as long as 12 years. Although expensive, balsamic vinegar has a very rich taste and is used in small quantities.

Raspberry – this is produced by letting chopped raspberries infuse in a good quality vinegar for a few days before straining. It can be diluted and drunk alone or used in dressings or fruit salads.

Yoghurt – this is made from fermented milk and is an extremely versatile dairy product. The yoghurt with the fewest calories is made with skimmed milk. It is relatively cheap and simple to make yoghurt at home by introducing the live culture to milk (see page 142).

Greek or Greek-style – this has a creamy consistency and a fat content of at least 8 per cent. It is often made with sheep's milk.

Index

Apple and berry strudel, 124
Apricot and passion fruit water ice, 114
Apricot, fig and coconut terrine, 116
Asparagus: asparagus and broccoli
    charlotte, 106
    asparagus and potato mayonnaise, 16
    morels stuffed with asparagus mousses,
    30
Aubergine gâteau with Provençale
    vegetables, 97
Avocado and sweetcorn soup, 36

Bananas: banana and sultana mousse, 112
    banana en papillote, 120
    sultana, walnut and banana bread, 145
Basmati rice timbale with coriander,
    truffle and pineapple dressing, 22
Bean and pepper lasagne, 92
Beef: fillet of beef with mango glaze, 69
Bread and fruit pudding with banana
    sauce, 116
Bread, basic, 143
Brill: brill and crab soufflé, 42
    brill with noodles and clams, 58

Carob: carob soufflé, 134
    carob tears, 134
Carrots: carrot and peanut terrine, 90
    carrot, scallop and coriander soup, 36

Celeriac: celeriac and wild mushroom
    terrine, 109
    celeriac spring rolls, 108
    celeriac, leek and sage soup, 38
    grilled corn-fed chicken with walnut
    and celeriac cakes, 73
Champneys apple crumble with honey-
    sweetened *fromage frais,* 117
Champneys bechamel, 141
Champneys *crème anglaise,* 142
Champneys fruit loaf, 145
Champneys gazpacho, 21
Champneys muesli, 142
Cherries: cherry and pistachio carob
    terrine, 134
    cherry soufflé, 134
    iced carob, cherry and pistachio terrine,
    126
Chicken: barbecued chicken chilli and
    pineapple wrapped in a cornflour
    pasty, 89
    chicken and scallop coulibiac, 32
    chicken leek mousse with beetroot
    salad, 17
    chicken stock, 138
    chicken, venison and wild mushroom
    terrine, 25
    grilled corn-fed chicken with walnut
    and celeriac cakes, 73
    stuffed breast with a tomato vinaigrette,
    70

sweet pepper, chicken, pineapple and chilli salad, 29

wild mushroom and chicken terrine, 18

Chickpea, olive and garlic soup, 33

Cod baked with wild mushrooms, tarragon and white wine, 56

Crab, beetroot and apple salad, 16

Délice of raspberries and nectarine, 119

Duck breast roasted with lentils and kumquat marmalade, 72

Duck liver mousse with sprouting lentils and smoked bacon, 66

Endive salad with balsamic honey dressing, 96

Feta cheese, leek, potato and yoghurt tartlets, 102

Fig, sultana and pecan pie, 128

Fish stock, 138

Frozen wild strawberry and yoghurt terrine, 110

Fruit and nut slice, 129

Gammon: smoked gammon brochettes, 80

Gurnard roasted with garlic and rosemary with gazpacho, 52

Honey tuile, 144

Ice cream, 143

Iced carob, cherry and pistachio terrine, 126

Kiwi and orange slice with sweet vinaigrette, 120

Lamb sweetbread ravioli, 44

Layers of cabbage, salmon and pike mousse with scampi tails, 61

Leek and herb sausages with pickled cabbage, 93

Leek, smoked goat's cheese and sesame seed salad, 28

Lemon and orange chiffon pie, 129

Lentil and wild mushroom bolognese, 94

Lobster and red pepper mousse, 14

Mackerel: grilled fillet with apple chutney, 53

mackerel, rhubarb and mange-tout terrine, 18

Mange-tout, mint and caviar soup, 37

Mango charlotte royale, 132

Melon lime soup, 20

Mexican bean soup, 37

Morels: morels stuffed with asparagus mousses, 30

salmon baked with samphire and morels, 55

Mushrooms: mushroom and tarragon soup, 48

mushroom ragout with grilled polenta, 49

Mussels: tagliatelle of mussels, 44

Onions: glazed onion and wild mushroom tartlets, 100

onion, fennel, apple and horseradish
    salad, 100
sardine and red onion terrine, 17
Orange and basil dressing, 137

Parrot fish cooked in an envelope, 60
Parsnip and chestnut soup, 40
Pasta: pasta, cured ham, rocket, garlic and
    basil salad, 101
    saffron, 141
    spinach, 141
    sweet, 141
    wholemeal, 140
Peaches: peach and lemon chutney, 140
    peach consommé with sweet ravioli, 125
    poached peaches served in a honey basket
        with rosehip tea and fig sorbet, 130
    poached peaches with cinnamon ice-
        cream, 133
Pheasant: pheasant and quail stuffed with
    apple and cranberry forcemeat, 88
    pheasant stuffed with truffle mousse and
        creamed fennel, 68
Pigeon: roasted baby pigeon with coriander
    and pearl barley dumplings, 70
    salad of marinated pigeon with walnuts
        and grapes, 41
Pineapple and almond soufflé, 122
Pork: marinated fillet of pork with sweet
    peppers, 84
    roast fillet of pork with apricot and
        onion, 82
Potato and parsley soup, 41
Pumpkin and pear pie, 117

Quail: galantine of smoked quail, 32
    pheasant and quail stuffed with apple and
        cranberry forcemeat, 88

quail with sweet pepper sauce and
    autumn vegetables, 81
roasted quail stuffed with chervil mousse,
    78

Raspberry and strawberry layer, 114
Red mullet: marinated with pressed leek
    terrine, 40
    red mullet with salad niçoise, 60
Red snapper cooked on a bed of aubergines
    with lemon vinaigrette, 57
Rhubarb charlotte, 113

Salad of smoked salmon, quail's eggs and
    samphire, 96
Salmon: layers of cabbage, salmon and pike
    mousse with scampi tails, 61
    salmon and leek mousse with salmon roe
        sauce, 28
    salmon baked with samphire and morels,
        55
    salmon poached in champagne served with
        cucumber and watercress salad, 64
Sardine and red onion terrine, 17
Scallops: scallop, bacon and mushroom
    salad with maple dressing, 48
    scallops poached in caraway and saffron,
        58
    warm salad of scallops with wild
        strawberry dressing, 46
Sea bass: marinated sea bass with pickled
    vegetables, 20
    sea bass grilled with sorrel and chives, 56
Smoked haddock tartare with artichoke
    terrine and lemon balm dressing, 24
Sultana, walnut and banana bread, 145
Swiss chard, beetroot, avocado and pecan
    nut salad, 26

Tomato and olive salad with mango
    dressing, 98
Tomato concasse, 137, 138
Trout wrapped in Chinese leaves with
    ginger and spring onion, 65
Tulip of passion fruit and apricot sorbet
    with fresh fruits, 121
Tuna: grilled with black-eyed beans and
    coriander, 63
Turbot steamed with baby spinach, red
    wine and thyme, 50

Veal: poached fillet of veal with broccoli
    mousse and carrot purée, 82
    roasted fillet of veal with roasted shallots
    and garlic with a Madeira sauce, 76
    veal stock, 139
    veal sweetbreads with leeks and
    watercress, 85
Vegetables: marinated grilled vegetables, 104
    vegetable and nut croquettes, 105
    vegetable stock, 139
Venison: saddle of venison roasted with

pistachio mousse, cabbage and juniper,
    77
Vinaigrette: basic, 136
    cucumber and ginger, 136
    strawberry, 137
    tomato, 136

Warm blueberry tartlets with lemon and
    cinnamon ice cream, 124
Wholemeal cinnamon muffins, 144
Wholemeal pastry, 144
Wild mushrooms: cod baked with
    wild mushrooms, tarragon and white
    wine, 56
    glazed onion and wild mushroom tartlets,
    100
    lentil and wild mushroom bolognese,
    94
    wild mushroom and chicken terrine, 18
    wild mushroom and lentil salad, 98

Yoghurt, 142

The author

ADAM PALMER is Master of Cuisine at Champneys, one of the world's finest health resorts. After working in a country house hotel in Hertfordshire and a city centre hotel in Birmingham, he joined Champneys as Sous Chef in 1987. He became Head Chef two years later.